Presented to

_____

By

_____

On the Occasion of

_____

Date

_____

PROMISES
of the
PROVERBS

Compiled by
Michael Beck

BARBOUR
PUBLISHING, INC.
Uhrichsville, Ohio

Published by Barbour Publishing, Inc.
        P.O. Box 719
        Uhrichsville, OH 44683
        http:\\www.barbourbooks.com

Member of the
Evangelical Christian
Publishers Association

Published in the United States of America.

Table of Contents

Introduction

The proverbs of Solomon the son of David, king of Israel; To know wisdom and instruction; to perceive the words of understanding; To receive the instruction of wisdom, justice, and judgment, and equity; To give subtilty to the simple, to the young man knowledge and discretion. A wise man will hear, and will increase learning; and a man of understanding shall attain unto wise counsels: To understand a proverb, and the interpretation; the words of the wise, and their dark sayings. The fear of the LORD is the beginning of knowledge: but fools despise wisdom and instruction.   *Proverbs 1:1–7*

Abomination

For the froward is abomination to the LORD: but his secret is with the righteous.

Proverbs 3:32

These six things doth the LORD hate: yea, seven are an abomination unto him: A proud look, a lying tongue, and hands that shed innocent blood, An heart that deviseth wicked imaginations, feet that be swift in running to mischief, A false witness that speaketh lies, and he that soweth discord among brethren.

Proverbs 6:16–19

Doth not wisdom cry? and understanding put forth her voice? . . .Unto you, O men, I call; and my voice is to the sons of man. . .Hear; for I will speak of excellent things; and the opening of my lips shall be right things. For my mouth shall speak truth; and wickedness is an abomination to my lips.

Proverbs 8:1,4,6–7

A false balance is abomination to the LORD: but a just weight is his delight.

Proverbs 11:1

They that are of a froward heart are abomination to the LORD: but such as are upright in their way are his delight.

Proverbs 11:20

Lying lips are abomination to the LORD: but they that deal truly are his delight. *Proverbs 12:22*

The desire accomplished is sweet to the soul: but it is abomination to fools to depart from evil. *Proverbs 13:19*

The sacrifice of the wicked is an abomination to the LORD: but the prayer of the upright is his delight. *Proverbs 15:8*

The way of the wicked is an abomination unto the LORD: but he loveth him that followeth after righteousness.
Proverbs 15:9

Every one that is proud in heart is an abomination to the LORD: though hand join in hand, he shall not be unpunished.
Proverbs 16:5

It is an abomination to kings to commit wickedness: for the throne is established by righteousness. *Proverbs 16:12*

He that justifieth the wicked, and he that condemneth the just, even they both are abomination to the LORD.
Proverbs 17:15

Divers weights, and divers measures, both of them are alike abomination to the LORD. *Proverbs 20:10*

Divers weights are an abomination unto the LORD; and a false balance is not good. *Proverbs 20:23*

The sacrifice of the wicked is abomination: how much more, when he bringeth it with a wicked mind?
Proverbs 21:27

The thought of foolishness is sin: and the scorner is an abomination to men. *Proverbs 24:9*

He that hateth dissembleth with his lips, and layeth up deceit within him; When he speaketh fair, believe him not: for there are seven abominations in his heart. Whose hatred is covered by deceit, his wickedness shall be shewed before the whole congregation. *Proverbs 26:24–26*

He that turneth away his ear from hearing the law, even his prayer shall be abomination. *Proverbs 28:9*

An unjust man is an abomination to the just: and he that is upright in the way is abomination to the wicked.
Proverbs 29:27

Anger

For jealousy is the rage of a man: therefore he will not spare in the day of vengeance.   *Proverbs 6:34*

Riches profit not in the day of wrath: but righteousness delivereth from death.   *Proverbs 11:4*

The desire of the righteous is only good: but the expectation of the wicked is wrath.   *Proverbs 11:23*

A fool's wrath is presently known: but a prudent man covereth shame.   *Proverbs 12:16*

He that is soon angry dealeth foolishly: and a man of wicked devices is hated.   *Proverbs 14:17*

He that is slow to wrath is of great understanding: but he that is hasty of spirit exalteth folly.   *Proverbs 14:29*

The king's favour is toward a wise servant: but his wrath is against him that causeth shame.   *Proverbs 14:35*

A soft answer turneth away wrath: but grievous words stir up anger.   *Proverbs 15:1*

A wrathful man stirreth up strife: but he that is slow to anger appeaseth strife. *Proverbs 15:18*

The wrath of a king is as messengers of death: but a wise man will pacify it. *Proverbs 16:14*

He that is slow to anger is better than the mighty; and he that ruleth his spirit than he that taketh a city.
Proverbs 16:32

The foolishness of man perverteth his way: and his heart fretteth against the Lord. *Proverbs 19:3*

The discretion of a man deferreth his anger; and it is his glory to pass over a transgression. *Proverbs 19:11*

The king's wrath is as the roaring of a lion; but his favour is as dew upon the grass. *Proverbs 19:12*

A man of great wrath shall suffer punishment: for if thou deliver him, yet thou must do it again. *Proverbs 19:19*

The fear of a king is as the roaring of a lion: whoso provoketh him to anger sinneth against his own soul. *Proverbs 20:2*

A gift in secret pacifieth anger: and a reward in the bosom strong wrath.   *Proverbs 21:14*

It is better to dwell in the wilderness, than with a contentious and an angry woman.   *Proverbs 21:19*

Proud and haughty scorner is his name, who dealeth in proud wrath.   *Proverbs 21:24*

He that soweth iniquity shall reap vanity: and the rod of his anger shall fail.   *Proverbs 22:8*

Make no friendship with an angry man; and with a furious man thou shalt not go: Lest thou learn his ways, and get a snare to thy soul.   *Proverbs 22:24–25*

Rejoice not when thine enemy falleth, and let not thine heart be glad when he stumbleth: Lest the Lord see it, and it displease him, and he turn away his wrath from him.

Proverbs 24:17–18

The north wind driveth away rain: so doth an angry countenance a backbiting tongue.   *Proverbs 25:23*

He that passeth by, and meddleth with strife belonging not to him, is like one that taketh a dog by the ears.

Proverbs 26:17

A stone is heavy, and the sand weighty; but a fool's wrath is heavier than them both. *Proverbs 27:3*

Wrath is cruel, and anger is outrageous; but who is able to stand before envy? *Proverbs 27:4*

Scornful men bring a city into a snare: but wise men turn away wrath. *Proverbs 29:8*

If a wise man contendeth with a foolish man, whether he rage or laugh, there is no rest. *Proverbs 29:9*

An angry man stirreth up strife, and a furious man aboundeth in transgression. *Proverbs 29:22*

Surely the churning of milk bringeth forth butter, and the wringing of the nose bringeth forth blood: so the forcing of wrath bringeth forth strife. *Proverbs 30:33*

Apathy

If thou forbear to deliver them that are drawn unto death, and those that are ready to be slain; If thou sayest, Behold, we knew it not; doth not he that pondereth the heart consider it? and he that keepeth thy soul, doth not he know it? and shall not he render to every man according to his works?

Proverbs 24:11–12

He that giveth unto the poor shall not lack: but he that hideth his eyes shall have many a curse.

Proverbs 28:27

The righteous considereth the cause of the poor: but the wicked regardeth not to know it.   *Proverbs 29:7*

Associations

My son, if sinners entice thee, consent thou not.
Proverbs 1:10

Enter not into the path of the wicked, and go not in the way of evil men. Avoid it, pass not by it, turn from it, and pass away. For they sleep not, except they have done mischief; and their sleep is taken away, unless they cause some to fall. For they eat the bread of wickedness, and drink the wine of violence.
Proverbs 4:14–17

Forsake the foolish, and live; and go in the way of understanding.
Proverbs 9:6

Though hand join in hand, the wicked shall not be unpunished: but the seed of the righteous shall be delivered.
Proverbs 11:21

He that tilleth his land shall be satisfied with bread: but he that followeth vain persons is void of understanding.
Proverbs 12:11

He that walketh with wise men shall be wise: but a companion of fools shall be destroyed.
Proverbs 13:20

Go from the presence of a foolish man, when thou perceivest not in him the lips of knowledge.   *Proverbs 14:7*

Every one that is proud in heart is an abomination to the LORD: though hand join in hand, he shall not be unpunished.   *Proverbs 16:5*

A violent man enticeth his neighbour, and leadeth him into the way that is not good. He shutteth his eyes to devise froward things: moving his lips he bringeth evil to pass.
                                              Proverbs 16:29–30

Make no friendship with an angry man; and with a furious man thou shalt not go: Lest thou learn his ways, and get a snare to thy soul.   *Proverbs 22:24–25*

Be not thou one of them that strike hands, or of them that are sureties for debts. If thou hast nothing to pay, why should he take away thy bed from under thee?
                                              Proverbs 22:26–27

Be not among winebibbers; among riotous eaters of flesh: For the drunkard and the glutton shall come to poverty: and drowsiness shall clothe a man with rags.
                                              Proverbs 23:20–21

Be not thou envious against evil men, neither desire to be with them. For their heart studieth destruction, and their lips talk of mischief.   *Proverbs 24:1–2*

Blessing

The curse of the LORD is in the house of the wicked: but he blesseth the habitation of the just.   *Proverbs 3:33*

Let thy fountain be blessed: and rejoice with the wife of thy youth.   *Proverbs 5:18*

Now therefore hearken unto me, O ye children: for blessed are they that keep my ways. Hear instruction, and be wise, and refuse it not. Blessed is the man that heareth me, watching daily at my gates, waiting at the posts of my doors. For whoso findeth me findeth life, and shall obtain favour of the LORD.   *Proverbs 8:32–35*

Blessings are upon the head of the just: but violence covereth the mouth of the wicked.   *Proverbs 10:6*

The memory of the just is blessed: but the name of the wicked shall rot.   *Proverbs 10:7*

The blessing of the LORD, it maketh rich, and he addeth no sorrow with it.   *Proverbs 10:22*

By the blessing of the upright the city is exalted: but it is overthrown by the mouth of the wicked.   *Proverbs 11:11*

He that withholdeth corn, the people shall curse him: but blessing shall be upon the head of him that selleth it.
Proverbs 11:26

The just man walketh in his integrity: his children are blessed after him.   *Proverbs 20:7*

An inheritance may be gotten hastily at the beginning; but the end thereof shall not be blessed.   *Proverbs 20:21*

He that hath a bountiful eye shall be blessed; for he giveth of his bread to the poor.   *Proverbs 22:9*

A faithful man shall abound with blessings: but he that maketh haste to be rich shall not be innocent.
Proverbs 28:20

There is a generation that curseth their father, and doth not bless their mother.   *Proverbs 30:11*

Brothers

These six things doth the LORD hate: yea, seven are an abomination unto him: A proud look, a lying tongue, and hands that shed innocent blood, An heart that deviseth wicked imaginations, feet that be swift in running to mischief, A false witness that speaketh lies, and he that soweth discord among brethren. *Proverbs 6:16–19*

A wise servant shall have rule over a son that causeth shame, and shall have part of the inheritance among the brethren. *Proverbs 17:2*

A friend loveth at all times, and a brother is born for adversity. *Proverbs 17:17*

A brother offended is harder to be won than a strong city: and their contentions are like the bars of a castle.
Proverbs 18:19

A man that hath friends must shew himself friendly: and there is a friend that sticketh closer than a brother.
Proverbs 18:24

Business

Treasures of wickedness profit nothing: but righteousness delivereth from death.   *Proverbs 10:2*

A false balance is abomination to the LORD: but a just weight is his delight.   *Proverbs 11:1*

He that tilleth his land shall be satisfied with bread: but he that followeth vain persons is void of understanding.
                    Proverbs 12:11

Wealth gotten by vanity shall be diminished: but he that gathereth by labour shall increase.   *Proverbs 13:11*

In all labour there is profit: but the talk of the lips tendeth only to penury.   *Proverbs 14:23*

Without counsel purposes are disappointed: but in the multitude of counsellors they are established.   *Proverbs 15:22*
He that laboureth laboureth for himself; for his mouth craveth it of him.   *Proverbs 16:26*

It is naught, it is naught, saith the buyer: but when he is gone his way, then he boasteth.   *Proverbs 20:14*

Take his garment that is surety for a stranger: and take a pledge of him for a strange woman.

Proverbs 20:16

The rich ruleth over the poor, and the borrower is servant to the lender. *Proverbs 22:7*

Seest thou a man diligent in his business? he shall stand before kings; he shall not stand before mean men.

Proverbs 22:29

Buy the truth, and sell it not; also wisdom, and instruction, and understanding. *Proverbs 23:23*

Prepare thy work without, and make it fit for thyself in the field; and afterwards build thine house. *Proverbs 24:27*

Children

My son, despise not the chastening of the LORD; neither be weary of his correction: For whom the LORD loveth he correcteth; even as a father the son in whom he delighteth.
Proverbs 3:11–12

He that spareth his rod hateth his son: but he that loveth him chasteneth him betimes. *Proverbs 13:24*

In the fear of the LORD is strong confidence: and his children shall have a place of refuge.
Proverbs 14:26

Children's children are the crown of old men; and the glory of children are their fathers. *Proverbs 17:6*

Chasten thy son while there is hope, and let not thy soul spare for his crying. *Proverbs 19:18*

The just man walketh in his integrity: his children are blessed after him. *Proverbs 20:7*

Even a child is known by his doings, whether his work be pure, and whether it be right. *Proverbs 20:11*

Train up a child in the way he should go: and when he is old, he will not depart from it. *Proverbs 22:6*

Foolishness is bound in the heart of a child; but the rod of correction shall drive it far from him. *Proverbs 22:15*

Withhold not correction from the child: for if thou beatest him with the rod, he shall not die. Thou shalt beat him with the rod, and shalt deliver his soul from hell.

Proverbs 23:13–14

The father of the righteous shall greatly rejoice: and he that begetteth a wise child shall have joy of him.

Proverbs 23:24

The rod and reproof give wisdom: but a child left to himself bringeth his mother to shame. *Proverbs 29:15*

He that delicately bringeth up his servant from a child shall have him become his son at the length.

Proverbs 29:21

Civic Affairs

When it goeth well with the righteous, the city rejoiceth: and when the wicked perish, there is shouting.

Proverbs 11:10

By the blessing of the upright the city is exalted: but it is overthrown by the mouth of the wicked.   *Proverbs 11:11*

He that withholdeth corn, the people shall curse him: but blessing shall be upon the head of him that selleth it.

Proverbs 11:26

Righteousness exalteth a nation: but sin is a reproach to any people.   *Proverbs 14:34*

A wise man scaleth the city of the mighty, and casteth down the strength of the confidence thereof.   *Proverbs 21:22*

He that saith unto the wicked, Thou art righteous; him shall the people curse, nations shall abhor him: But to them that rebuke him shall be delight, and a good blessing shall come upon them.   *Proverbs 24:24–25*

For the transgression of a land many are the princes thereof: but by a man of understanding and knowledge the state thereof shall be prolonged.   *Proverbs 28:2*

As a roaring lion, and a ranging bear; so is a wicked ruler over the poor people.   *Proverbs 28:15*

When the righteous are in authority, the people rejoice: but when the wicked beareth rule, the people mourn.
                    Proverbs 29:2

The king by judgment establisheth the land: but he that receiveth gifts overthroweth it.   *Proverbs 29:4*

Scornful men bring a city into a snare: but wise men turn away wrath.   *Proverbs 29:8*

If a ruler hearken to lies, all his servants are wicked.
                    Proverbs 29:12

Confidence

Be not afraid of sudden fear, neither of the desolation of the wicked, when it cometh. For the LORD shall be thy confidence, and shall keep thy foot from being taken.

Proverbs 3:25–26

He that walketh uprightly walketh surely: but he that perverteth his ways shall be known.   *Proverbs 10:9*

The rich man's wealth is his strong city: the destruction of the poor is their poverty.   *Proverbs 10:15*

He that trusteth in his riches shall fall: but the righteous shall flourish as a branch.   *Proverbs 11:28*

A wise man feareth, and departeth from evil: but the fool rageth, and is confident.   *Proverbs 14:16*

In the fear of the LORD is strong confidence: and his children shall have a place of refuge.   *Proverbs 14:26*

A wise man scaleth the city of the mighty, and casteth down the strength of the confidence thereof.   *Proverbs 21:22*

Counsel

A wise man will hear, and will increase learning; and a man of understanding shall attain unto wise counsels.

Proverbs 1:5

I wisdom dwell with prudence, and find out knowledge of witty inventions. . .Counsel is mine, and sound wisdom: I am understanding; I have strength.   *Proverbs 8:12,14*

Where no counsel is, the people fall: but in the multitude of counsellors there is safety.   *Proverbs 11:14*

The thoughts of the righteous are right: but the counsels of the wicked are deceit.   *Proverbs 12:5*

The way of a fool is right in his own eyes: but he that hearkeneth unto counsel is wise.   *Proverbs 12:15*

Without counsel purposes are disappointed: but in the multitude of counsellors they are established.   *Proverbs 15:22*

Hear counsel, and receive instruction, that thou mayest be wise in thy latter end.   *Proverbs 19:20*

There are many devices in a man's heart; nevertheless the counsel of the LORD, that shall stand.   *Proverbs 19:21*

Counsel in the heart of man is like deep water; but a man of understanding will draw it out.   *Proverbs 20:5*

Every purpose is established by counsel: and with good advice make war.   *Proverbs 20:18*

There is no wisdom nor understanding nor counsel against the LORD.   *Proverbs 21:30*

Have not I written to thee excellent things in counsels and knowledge, That I might make thee know the certainty of the words of truth; that thou mightest answer the words of truth to them that send unto thee?   *Proverbs 22:20–21*

Curses

The curse of the LORD is in the house of the wicked: but he blesseth the habitation of the just. *Proverbs 3:33*

He that withholdeth corn, the people shall curse him: but blessing shall be upon the head of him that selleth it.
Proverbs 11:26

Whoso curseth his father or his mother, his lamp shall be put out in obscure darkness. *Proverbs 20:20*

He that saith unto the wicked, Thou art righteous; him shall the people curse, nations shall abhor him *Proverbs 24:24*

As the bird by wandering, as the swallow by flying, so the curse causeless shall not come. *Proverbs 26:2*

He that blesseth his friend with a loud voice, rising early in the morning, it shall be counted a curse to him.
Proverbs 27:14

He that giveth unto the poor shall not lack: but he that hideth his eyes shall have many a curse. *Proverbs 28:27*

Death

For the lips of a strange woman drop as an honeycomb, and her mouth is smoother than oil: But her end is bitter as wormwood, sharp as a twoedged sword. Her feet go down to death; her steps take hold on hell.   *Proverbs 5:3–5*

His own iniquities shall take the wicked himself, and he shall be holden with the cords of his sins. He shall die without instruction; and in the greatness of his folly he shall go astray.   *Proverbs 5:22–23*

For whoso findeth me findeth life, and shall obtain favour of the Lord. But he that sinneth against me wrongeth his own soul: all they that hate me love death.

Proverbs 8:35–36

A foolish woman is clamorous: she is simple, and knoweth nothing. For she sitteth at the door of her house, on a seat in the high places of the city, To call passengers who go right on their ways: Whoso is simple, let him turn in hither: and as for him that wanteth understanding, she saith to him, Stolen waters are sweet, and bread eaten in secret is pleasant. But he knoweth not that the dead are there; and that her guests are in the depths of hell.   *Proverbs 9:13–18*

Treasures of wickedness profit nothing: but righteousness delivereth from death.   *Proverbs 10:2*

Riches profit not in the day of wrath: but righteousness delivereth from death.   *Proverbs 11:4*

When a wicked man dieth, his expectation shall perish: and the hope of unjust men perisheth.   *Proverbs 11:7*

As righteousness tendeth to life: so he that pursueth evil pursueth it to his own death.   *Proverbs 11:19*

In the way of righteousness is life; and in the pathway thereof there is no death.   *Proverbs 12:28*

The law of the wise is a fountain of life, to depart from the snares of death.   *Proverbs 13:14*

There is a way which seemeth right unto a man, but the end thereof are the ways of death.   *Proverbs 14:12*

The fear of the LORD is a fountain of life, to depart from the snares of death.   *Proverbs 14:27*

The wicked is driven away in his wickedness: but the righteous hath hope in his death. *Proverbs 14:32*

Correction is grievous unto him that forsaketh the way: and he that hateth reproof shall die. *Proverbs 15:10*

The wrath of a king is as messengers of death: but a wise man will pacify it. *Proverbs 16:14*

Death and life are in the power of the tongue: and they that love it shall eat the fruit thereof. *Proverbs 18:21*

He that keepeth the commandment keepeth his own soul; but he that despiseth his ways shall die. *Proverbs 19:16*

The getting of treasures by a lying tongue is a vanity tossed to and fro of them that seek death. *Proverbs 21:6*

The man that wandereth out of the way of understanding shall remain in the congregation of the dead.

Proverbs 21:16

Deceit

The wicked worketh a deceitful work: but to him that soweth righteousness shall be a sure reward.

Proverbs 11:18

The thoughts of the righteous are right: but the counsels of the wicked are deceit.

Proverbs 12:5

He that speaketh truth sheweth forth righteousness: but a false witness deceit.

Proverbs 12:17

Deceit is in the heart of them that imagine evil: but to the counsellors of peace is joy.

Proverbs 12:20

The wisdom of the prudent is to understand his way: but the folly of fools is deceit.

Proverbs 14:8

A true witness delivereth souls: but a deceitful witness speaketh lies.

Proverbs 14:25

A wicked doer giveth heed to false lips; and a liar giveth ear to a naughty tongue.

Proverbs 17:4

Wine is a mocker, strong drink is raging: and whosoever is deceived thereby is not wise.

Proverbs 20:1

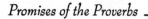

Bread of deceit is sweet to a man; but afterwards his mouth shall be filled with gravel. *Proverbs 20:17*

When thou sittest to eat with a ruler, consider diligently what is before thee: And put a knife to thy throat, if thou be a man given to appetite. Be not desirous of his dainties: for they are deceitful meat. Labour not to be rich: cease from thine own wisdom. Wilt thou set thine eyes upon that which is not? for riches certainly make themselves wings; they fly away as an eagle toward heaven. Eat thou not the bread of him that hath an evil eye, neither desire thou his dainty meats: For as he thinketh in his heart, so is he: Eat and drink, saith he to thee; but his heart is not with thee. The morsel which thou hast eaten shalt thou vomit up, and lose thy sweet words. *Proverbs 23:1–8*

Be not a witness against thy neighbour without cause; and deceive not with thy lips. Say not, I will do so to him as he hath done to me: I will render to the man according to his work. *Proverbs 24:28–29*

Whoso boasteth himself of a false gift is like clouds and wind without rain. *Proverbs 25:14*

As a mad man who casteth firebrands, arrows, and death, So is the man that deceiveth his neighbour, and saith, Am not I in sport? *Proverbs 26:18–19*

Burning lips and a wicked heart are like a potsherd covered with silver dross. He that hateth dissembleth with his lips, and layeth up deceit within him; When he speaketh fair, believe him not: for there are seven abominations in his heart. Whose hatred is covered by deceit, his wickedness shall be shewed before the whole congregation.

Proverbs 26:23–26

Faithful are the wounds of a friend; but the kisses of an enemy are deceitful. *Proverbs 27:6*

The poor and the deceitful man meet together: the LORD lighteneth both their eyes. *Proverbs 29:13*

Favour is deceitful, and beauty is vain: but a woman that feareth the LORD, she shall be praised. *Proverbs 31:30*

Delight

My son, despise not the chastening of the LORD; neither be weary of his correction: For whom the LORD loveth he correcteth; even as a father the son in whom he delighteth.

Proverbs 3:11–12

A false balance is abomination to the LORD: but a just weight is his delight. *Proverbs 11:1*

They that are of a froward heart are abomination to the LORD: but such as are upright in their way are his delight.

Proverbs 11:20

Lying lips are abomination to the LORD: but they that deal truly are his delight. *Proverbs 12:22*

The sacrifice of the wicked is an abomination to the LORD: but the prayer of the upright is his delight. *Proverbs 15:8*

Righteous lips are the delight of kings; and they love him that speaketh right. *Proverbs 16:13*

A fool hath no delight in understanding, but that his heart may discover itself. *Proverbs 18:2*

Delight is not seemly for a fool; much less for a servant to have rule over princes.   *Proverbs 19:10*

These things also belong to the wise. It is not good to have respect of persons in judgment. He that saith unto the wicked, Thou art righteous; him shall the people curse, nations shall abhor him: But to them that rebuke him shall be delight, and a good blessing shall come upon them.
                                                    Proverbs 24:23–25

Correct thy son, and he shall give thee rest; yea, he shall give delight unto thy soul.   *Proverbs 29:17*

Deliverance

Treasures of wickedness profit nothing: but righteousness delivereth from death.   *Proverbs 10:2*

Riches profit not in the day of wrath: but righteousness delivereth from death.   *Proverbs 11:4*

The righteous is delivered out of trouble, and the wicked cometh in his stead.   *Proverbs 11:8*

Though hand join in hand, the wicked shall not be unpunished: but the seed of the righteous shall be delivered.
Proverbs 11:21

The words of the wicked are to lie in wait for blood: but the mouth of the upright shall deliver them.   *Proverbs 12:6*

A true witness delivereth souls: but a deceitful witness speaketh lies.   *Proverbs 14:25*

A man of great wrath shall suffer punishment: for if thou deliver him, yet thou must do it again.   *Proverbs 19:19*

Say not thou, I will recompense evil; but wait on the LORD, and he shall save thee.   *Proverbs 20:22*

Withhold not correction from the child: for if thou beatest him with the rod, he shall not die. Thou shalt beat him with the rod, and shalt deliver his soul from hell.
Proverbs 23:13–14

If thou forbear to deliver them that are drawn unto death, and those that are ready to be slain; If thou sayest, Behold, we knew it not; doth not he that pondereth the heart consider it? and he that keepeth thy soul, doth not he know it? and shall not he render to every man according to his works?
Proverbs 24:11–12

Whoso walketh uprightly shall be saved: but he that is perverse in his ways shall fall at once.   *Proverbs 28:18*

He that trusteth in his own heart is a fool: but whoso walketh wisely, he shall be delivered.   *Proverbs 28:26*

Desire

Happy is the man that findeth wisdom, and the man that getteth understanding. For the merchandise of it is better than the merchandise of silver, and the gain thereof than fine gold. She is more precious than rubies: and all the things thou canst desire are not to be compared unto her.
Proverbs 3:13–15

Doth not wisdom cry? and understanding put forth her voice? . . .Unto you, O men, I call; and my voice is to the sons of man. . .Receive my instruction, and not silver; and knowledge rather than choice gold. For wisdom is better than rubies; and all the things that may be desired are not to be compared to it.
Proverbs 8:1,4,10–11

The fear of the wicked, it shall come upon him: but the desire of the righteous shall be granted.
Proverbs 10:24

The desire of the righteous is only good: but the expectation of the wicked is wrath.
Proverbs 11:23

Hope deferred maketh the heart sick: but when the desire cometh, it is a tree of life.
Proverbs 13:12

The desire accomplished is sweet to the soul: but it is abomination to fools to depart from evil. *Proverbs 13:19*

Through desire a man, having separated himself, seeketh and intermeddleth with all wisdom. *Proverbs 18:1*

The desire of a man is his kindness: and a poor man is better than a liar. *Proverbs 19:22*

The soul of the wicked desireth evil: his neighbour findeth no favour in his eyes. *Proverbs 21:10*

There is treasure to be desired and oil in the dwelling of the wise; but a foolish man spendeth it up. *Proverbs 21:20*

The desire of the slothful killeth him; for his hands refuse to labour. He coveteth greedily all the day long: but the righteous giveth and spareth not. *Proverbs 21:25–26*

When thou sittest to eat with a ruler, consider diligently what is before thee: And put a knife to thy throat, if thou be a man given to appetite. Be not desirous of his dainties: for they are deceitful meat. *Proverbs 23:1–3*

Destruction

For the turning away of the simple shall slay them, and the prosperity of fools shall destroy them.   *Proverbs 1:32*

My son, let not them depart from thine eyes: keep sound wisdom and discretion: So shall they be life unto thy soul, and grace to thy neck. Then shalt thou walk in thy way safely, and thy foot shall not stumble. When thou liest down, thou shalt not be afraid: yea, thou shalt lie down, and thy sleep shall be sweet. Be not afraid of sudden fear, neither of the desolation of the wicked, when it cometh. For the LORD shall be thy confidence, and shall keep thy foot from being taken.   *Proverbs 3:21–26*

A naughty person, a wicked man, walketh with a froward mouth. He winketh with his eyes, he speaketh with his feet, he teacheth with his fingers; Frowardness is in his heart, he deviseth mischief continually; he soweth discord. Therefore shall his calamity come suddenly; suddenly shall he be broken without remedy.   *Proverbs 6:12–15*

Wise men lay up knowledge: but the mouth of the foolish is near destruction.   *Proverbs 10:14*

The rich man's wealth is his strong city: the destruction of the poor is their poverty.   *Proverbs 10:15*

The way of the LORD is strength to the upright: but destruction shall be to the workers of iniquity.   *Proverbs 10:29*

The integrity of the upright shall guide them: but the perverseness of transgressors shall destroy them.

Proverbs 11:3

The righteousness of the perfect shall direct his way: but the wicked shall fall by his own wickedness.

Proverbs 11:5

An hypocrite with his mouth destroyeth his neighbour: but through knowledge shall the just be delivered.

Proverbs 11:9

Where no counsel is, the people fall: but in the multitude of counsellors there is safety.   *Proverbs 11:14*

He that trusteth in his riches shall fall: but the righteous shall flourish as a branch.   *Proverbs 11:28*

The wicked are overthrown, and are not: but the house of the righteous shall stand.   *Proverbs 12:7*

He that keepeth his mouth keepeth his life: but he that openeth wide his lips shall have destruction.

Proverbs 13:3

Righteousness keepeth him that is upright in the way: but wickedness overthroweth the sinner.   *Proverbs 13:6*

Whoso despiseth the word shall be destroyed: but he that feareth the commandment shall be rewarded.
Proverbs 13:13

He that walketh with wise men shall be wise: but a companion of fools shall be destroyed.   *Proverbs 13:20*

Much food is in the tillage of the poor: but there is that is destroyed for want of judgment.   *Proverbs 13:23*

The house of the wicked shall be overthrown: but the tabernacle of the upright shall flourish.   *Proverbs 14:11*

In the multitude of people is the king's honour: but in the want of people is the destruction of the prince.
Proverbs 14:28

Hell and destruction are before the LORD: how much more then the hearts of the children of men?   *Proverbs 15:11*

The LORD will destroy the house of the proud: but he will establish the border of the widow.   *Proverbs 15:25*

Pride goeth before destruction, and an haughty spirit before a fall.
Proverbs 16:18

He loveth transgression that loveth strife: and he that exalteth his gate seeketh destruction.
Proverbs 17:19

A fool's mouth is his destruction, and his lips are the snare of his soul.
Proverbs 18:7

Before destruction the heart of man is haughty, and before honour is humility.
Proverbs 18:12

The robbery of the wicked shall destroy them; because they refuse to do judgment.
Proverbs 21:7

The righteous man wisely considereth the house of the wicked: but God overthroweth the wicked for their wickedness.
Proverbs 21:12

It is joy to the just to do judgment: but destruction shall be to the workers of iniquity.
Proverbs 21:15

The mouth of strange women is a deep pit: he that is abhorred of the LORD shall fall therein.
Proverbs 22:14

Be not thou envious against evil men, neither desire to be with them. For their heart studieth destruction, and their lips talk of mischief. *Proverbs 24:1–2*

Rejoice not when thine enemy falleth, and let not thine heart be glad when he stumbleth: *Proverbs 24:17*

My son, fear thou the LORD and the king: and meddle not with them that are given to change: For their calamity shall rise suddenly; and who knoweth the ruin of them both? *Proverbs 24:21–22*

Whoso diggeth a pit shall fall therein: and he that rolleth a stone, it will return upon him. *Proverbs 26:27*

A lying tongue hateth those that are afflicted by it; and a flattering mouth worketh ruin. *Proverbs 26:28*

Hell and destruction are never full; so the eyes of man are never satisfied. *Proverbs 27:20*

Whoso causeth the righteous to go astray in an evil way, he shall fall himself into his own pit: but the upright shall have good things in possession. *Proverbs 28:10*

Whoso walketh uprightly shall be saved: but he that is perverse in his ways shall fall at once. *Proverbs 28:18*

Whoso robbeth his father or his mother, and saith, It is no transgression; the same is the companion of a destroyer.

Proverbs 28:24

When the wicked rise, men hide themselves: but when they perish, the righteous increase. *Proverbs 28:28*

He, that being often reproved hardeneth his neck, shall suddenly be destroyed, and that without remedy.

Proverbs 29:1

The king by judgment establisheth the land: but he that receiveth gifts overthroweth it. *Proverbs 29:4*

When the wicked are multiplied, transgression increaseth: but the righteous shall see their fall. *Proverbs 29:16*

Where there is no vision, the people perish: but he that keepeth the law, happy is he. *Proverbs 29:18*

Diligence

Keep thy heart with all diligence; for out of it are the issues of life. *Proverbs 4:23*

Go to the ant, thou sluggard; consider her ways, and be wise: Which having no guide, overseer, or ruler Provideth her meat in the summer, and gathereth her food in the harvest. *Proverbs 6:6–8*

He becometh poor that dealeth with a slack hand: but the hand of the diligent maketh rich. *Proverbs 10:4*

He that gathereth in summer is a wise son: but he that sleepeth in harvest is a son that causeth shame. *Proverbs 10:5*

He that diligently seeketh good procureth favour: but he that seeketh mischief, it shall come unto him. *Proverbs 11:27*

The hand of the diligent shall bear rule: but the slothful shall be under tribute. *Proverbs 12:24*

The slothful man roasteth not that which he took in hunting: but the substance of a diligent man is precious. *Proverbs 12:27*

The soul of the sluggard desireth, and hath nothing: but the soul of the diligent shall be made fat.   *Proverbs 13:4*

The thoughts of the diligent tend only to plenteousness; but of every one that is hasty only to want.   *Proverbs 21:5*

Seest thou a man diligent in his business? he shall stand before kings; he shall not stand before mean men.

Proverbs 22:29

Be thou diligent to know the state of thy flocks, and look well to thy herds.   *Proverbs 27:23*

Evil

For the turning away of the simple shall slay them, and the prosperity of fools shall destroy them. But whoso hearkeneth unto me shall dwell safely, and shall be quiet from fear of evil.   *Proverbs 1:32–33*

When wisdom entereth into thine heart, and knowledge is pleasant unto thy soul; Discretion shall preserve thee, understanding shall keep thee: To deliver thee from the way of the evil man, from the man that speaketh froward things; Who leave the paths of uprightness, to walk in the ways of darkness; Who rejoice to do evil, and delight in the frowardness of the wicked; Whose ways are crooked, and they froward in their paths.   *Proverbs 2:10–15*

Be not wise in thine own eyes: fear the LORD, and depart from evil. It shall be health to thy navel, and marrow to thy bones.   *Proverbs 3:7–8*

Enter not into the path of the wicked, and go not in the way of evil men. Avoid it, pass not by it, turn from it, and pass away. For they sleep not, except they have done mischief; and their sleep is taken away, unless they cause some to fall. For they eat the bread of wickedness, and drink the wine of violence.   *Proverbs 4:14–17*

Ponder the path of thy feet, and let all thy ways be established. Turn not to the right hand nor to the left: remove thy foot from evil. *Proverbs 4:26–27*

The fear of the LORD is to hate evil: pride, and arrogancy, and the evil way, and the froward mouth, do I hate.
Proverbs 8:13

As righteousness tendeth to life: so he that pursueth evil pursueth it to his own death. *Proverbs 11:19*

Deceit is in the heart of them that imagine evil: but to the counsellors of peace is joy. *Proverbs 12:20*

There shall no evil happen to the just: but the wicked shall be filled with mischief. *Proverbs 12:21*

The desire accomplished is sweet to the soul: but it is abomination to fools to depart from evil. *Proverbs 13:19*

Evil pursueth sinners: but to the righteous good shall be repayed. *Proverbs 13:21*

A wise man feareth, and departeth from evil: but the fool rageth, and is confident. *Proverbs 14:16*

The evil bow before the good; and the wicked at the gates of the righteous. *Proverbs 14:19*

Do they not err that devise evil? but mercy and truth shall be to them that devise good. *Proverbs 14:22*

The eyes of the LORD are in every place, beholding the evil and the good. *Proverbs 15:3*

All the days of the afflicted are evil: but he that is of a merry heart hath a continual feast. *Proverbs 15:15*

The heart of the righteous studieth to answer: but the mouth of the wicked poureth out evil things. *Proverbs 15:28*

The LORD hath made all things for himself: yea, even the wicked for the day of evil. *Proverbs 16:4*

By mercy and truth iniquity is purged: and by the fear of the LORD men depart from evil. *Proverbs 16:6*

The highway of the upright is to depart from evil: he that keepeth his way preserveth his soul. *Proverbs 16:17*

An ungodly man diggeth up evil: and in his lips there is as a burning fire. *Proverbs 16:27*

A violent man enticeth his neighbour, and leadeth him into the way that is not good. He shutteth his eyes to devise froward things: moving his lips he bringeth evil to pass.

Proverbs 16:29–30

An evil man seeketh only rebellion: therefore a cruel messenger shall be sent against him. *Proverbs 17:11*

Whoso rewardeth evil for good, evil shall not depart from his house. *Proverbs 17:13*

The fear of the LORD tendeth to life: and he that hath it shall abide satisfied; he shall not be visited with evil.

Proverbs 19:23

A king that sitteth in the throne of judgment scattereth away all evil with his eyes. *Proverbs 20:8*

Say not thou, I will recompense evil; but wait on the LORD, and he shall save thee. *Proverbs 20:22*

The blueness of a wound cleanseth away evil: so do stripes the inward parts of the belly. *Proverbs 20:30*

The soul of the wicked desireth evil: his neighbour findeth no favour in his eyes. *Proverbs 21:10*

A prudent man foreseeth the evil, and hideth himself: but the simple pass on, and are punished.

Proverbs 22:3

Be not thou envious against evil men, neither desire to be with them.   *Proverbs 24:1*

He that deviseth to do evil shall be called a mischievous person.   *Proverbs 24:8*

Fret not thyself because of evil men, neither be thou envious at the wicked; For there shall be no reward to the evil man; the candle of the wicked shall be put out.

Proverbs 24:19–20

Evil men understand not judgment: but they that seek the LORD understand all things.   *Proverbs 28:5*

Expectation

The hope of the righteous shall be gladness: but the expectation of the wicked shall perish.   *Proverbs 10:28*

When a wicked man dieth his expectation shall perish: and the hope of unjust men perisheth.   *Proverbs 11:7*

The desire of the righteous is only good: but the expectation of the wicked is wrath.   *Proverbs 11:23*

Let not thine heart envy sinners: but be thou in the fear of the LORD all the day long. For surely there is an end; and thine expectation shall not be cut off.   *Proverbs 23:17–18*

My son, eat thou honey, because it is good; and the honeycomb, which is sweet to thy taste: So shall the knowledge of wisdom be unto thy soul: when thou has found it, then there shall be a reward, and thy expectation shall not be cut off.
          Proverbs 24:13–14

Faithfulness

A talebearer revealeth secrets: but he that is of a faithful spirit concealeth the matter. *Proverbs 11:13*

A wicked messenger falleth into mischief: but a faithful ambassador is health. *Proverbs 13:17*

A friend loveth at all times, and a brother is born for adversity. *Proverbs 17:17*

Most men will proclaim every one his own goodness: but a faithful man who can find? *Proverbs 20:6*

As the cold of snow in the time of harvest, so is a faithful messenger to them that send him: for he refresheth the soul of his masters. *Proverbs 25:13*

Faithful are the wounds of a friend; but the kisses of an enemy are deceitful. *Proverbs 27:6*

Thine own friend, and thy father's friend, forsake not; neither go into thy brother's house in the day of thy calamity: for better is a neighbour that is near than a brother far off. *Proverbs 27:10*

Fathers

My son, hear the instruction of thy father, and forsake not the law of thy mother: For they shall be an ornament of grace unto thy head, and chains about thy neck.

Proverbs 1:8–9

My son, despise not the chastening of the LORD; neither be weary of his correction: For whom the LORD loveth he correcteth; even as a father the son in whom he delighteth.

Proverbs 3:11–12

Hear, ye children, the instruction of a father, and attend to know understanding. For I give you good doctrine, forsake ye not my law. For I was my father's son, tender and only beloved in the sight of my mother. He taught me also, and said unto me, Let thine heart retain my words: keep my commandments, and live. *Proverbs 4:1–4*

My son, keep thy father's commandment, and forsake not the law of thy mother: Bind them continually upon thine heart, and tie them about thy neck. When thou goest, it shall lead thee; when thou sleepest, it shall keep thee; and when thou awakest, it shall talk with thee. *Proverbs 6:20–22*

A wise son maketh a glad father: but a foolish son is the heaviness of his mother. *Proverbs 10:1*

A wise son heareth his father's instruction: but a scorner heareth not rebuke.   *Proverbs 13:1*

He that spareth his rod hateth his son: but he that loveth him chasteneth him betimes.   *Proverbs 13:24*

A fool despiseth his father's instruction: but he that regardeth reproof is prudent.   *Proverbs 15:5*

A wise son maketh a glad father: but a foolish man despiseth his mother.   *Proverbs 15:20*

Children's children are the crown of old men; and the glory of children are their fathers.   *Proverbs 17:6*

He that begetteth a fool doeth it to his sorrow: and the father of a fool hath no joy.   *Proverbs 17:21*

A foolish son is a grief to his father, and bitterness to her that bare him.   *Proverbs 17:25*

A foolish son is the calamity of his father: and the contentions of a wife are a continual dropping.
                                                  Proverbs 19:13

House and riches are the inheritance of fathers: and a prudent wife is from the LORD.   *Proverbs 19:14*

He that wasteth his father, and chaseth away his mother, is a son that causeth shame, and bringeth reproach.

Proverbs 19:26

Whoso curseth his father or his mother, his lamp shall be put out in obscure darkness. *Proverbs 20:20*

Remove not the ancient landmark, which thy fathers have set. *Proverbs 22:28*

Hearken unto thy father that begat thee, and despise not thy mother when she is old. *Proverbs 23:22*

The father of the righteous shall greatly rejoice: and he that begetteth a wise child shall have joy of him. Thy father and thy mother shall be glad, and she that bare thee shall rejoice. *Proverbs 23:24–25*

Whoso keepeth the law is a wise son: but he that is a companion of riotous men shameth his father. *Proverbs 28:7*

Whoso robbeth his father or his mother, and saith, It is no transgression; the same is the companion of a destroyer.

Proverbs 28:24

Whoso loveth wisdom rejoiceth his father: but he that keepeth company with harlots spendeth his substance.

Proverbs 29:3

Favor

Let not mercy and truth forsake thee: bind them about thy neck; write them upon the table of thine heart: So shalt thou find favour and good understanding in the sight of God and man.   *Proverbs 3:3–4*

For whoso findeth me findeth life, and shall obtain favour of the LORD. But he that sinneth against me wrongeth his own soul: all they that hate me love death.   *Proverbs 8:35–36*

He that diligently seeketh good procureth favour: but he that seeketh mischief, it shall come unto him.
Proverbs 11:27

A good man obtaineth favour of the LORD: but a man of wicked devices will he condemn.   *Proverbs 12:2*

Good understanding giveth favour: but the way of transgressors is hard.   *Proverbs 13:15*

Fools make a mock at sin: but among the righteous there is favour.   *Proverbs 14:9*

The king's favour is toward a wise servant: but his wrath is against him that causeth shame.   *Proverbs 14:35*

In the light of the king's countenance is life; and his favour is as a cloud of the latter rain. *Proverbs 16:15*

Whoso findeth a wife findeth a good thing, and obtaineth favour of the LORD. *Proverbs 18:22*

Many will intreat the favour of the prince: and every man is a friend to him that giveth gifts. *Proverbs 19:6*

The king's wrath is as the roaring of a lion; but his favour is as dew upon the grass. *Proverbs 19:12*

The soul of the wicked desireth evil: his neighbour findeth no favour in his eyes. *Proverbs 21:10*

A good name is rather to be chosen than great riches, and loving favour rather than silver and gold. *Proverbs 22:1*

He that rebuketh a man afterwards shall find more favour than he that flattereth with the tongue. *Proverbs 28:23*

Many seek the ruler's favour; but every man's judgment cometh from the LORD. *Proverbs 29:26*

Fear of the Lord

The fear of the LORD is the beginning of knowledge: but fools despise wisdom and instruction.   *Proverbs 1:7*

My son, if thou wilt receive my words, and hide my commandments with thee; So that thou incline thine ear unto wisdom, and apply thine heart to understanding; Yea, if thou criest after knowledge, and liftest up thy voice for understanding; If thou seekest her as silver, and searchest for her as for hid treasures; Then shalt thou understand the fear of the LORD, and find the knowledge of God.   *Proverbs 2:1–5*

Be not wise in thine own eyes: fear the LORD, and depart from evil. It shall be health to thy navel, and marrow to thy bones.   *Proverbs 3:7–8*

The fear of the LORD is to hate evil: pride, and arrogancy, and the evil way, and the froward mouth, do I hate.
              Proverbs 8:13

The fear of the LORD is the beginning of wisdom: and the knowledge of the holy is understanding. For by me thy days shall be multiplied, and the years of thy life shall be increased.   *Proverbs 9:10–11*

The fear of the LORD prolongeth days: but the years of the wicked shall be shortened.   *Proverbs 10:27*

He that walketh in his uprightness feareth the LORD: but he that is perverse in his ways despiseth him.

Proverbs 14:2

In the fear of the LORD is strong confidence: and his children shall have a place of refuge.   *Proverbs 14:26*

The fear of the LORD is a fountain of life, to depart from the snares of death.   *Proverbs 14:27*

Better is little with the fear of the LORD than great treasure and trouble therewith.   *Proverbs 15:16*

The fear of the LORD is the instruction of wisdom; and before honour is humility.   *Proverbs 15:33*

The fear of the LORD tendeth to life: and he that hath it shall abide satisfied; he shall not be visited with evil.

Proverbs 19:23

By humility and the fear of the LORD are riches, and honour, and life.   *Proverbs 22:4*

Let not thine heart envy sinners: but be thou in the fear of the LORD all the day long.   *Proverbs 23:17*

Flattery

When wisdom entereth into thine heart, and knowledge is pleasant unto thy soul; Discretion shall preserve thee, understanding shall keep thee. . .To deliver thee from the strange woman, even from the stranger which flattereth with her words   *Proverbs 2:10–11,16*

For the commandment is a lamp; and the law is light; and reproofs of instruction are the way of life: To keep thee from the evil woman, from the flattery of the tongue of a strange woman.   *Proverbs 6:23–24*

My son, keep my words, and lay up my commandments with thee. Keep my commandments, and live; and my law as the apple of thine eye. . .That they may keep thee from the strange woman, from the stranger which flattereth with her words.   *Proverbs 7:1–2,5*

He that goeth about as a talebearer revealeth secrets: therefore meddle not with him that flattereth with his lips.
                         Proverbs 20:19

As he that bindeth a stone in a sling, so is he that giveth honour to a fool.   *Proverbs 26:8*

Folly

His own iniquities shall take the wicked himself, and he shall be holden with the cords of his sins. He shall die without instruction; and in the greatness of his folly he shall go astray. *Proverbs 5:22,23*

Every prudent man dealeth with knowledge: but a fool layeth open his folly. *Proverbs 13:16*

The wisdom of the prudent is to understand his way: but the folly of fools is deceit. *Proverbs 14:8*

The simple inherit folly: but the prudent are crowned with knowledge. *Proverbs 14:18*

The crown of the wise is their riches: but the foolishness of fools is folly. *Proverbs 14:24*

He that is slow to wrath is of great understanding: but he that is hasty of spirit exalteth folly. *Proverbs 14:29*

Folly is joy to him that is destitute of wisdom: but a man of understanding walketh uprightly. *Proverbs 15:21*

Understanding is a wellspring of life unto him that hath it: but the instruction of fools is folly.   *Proverbs 16:22*

Let a bear robbed of her whelps meet a man, rather than a fool in his folly.   *Proverbs 17:12*

He that answereth a matter before he heareth it, it is folly and shame unto him.   *Proverbs 18:13*

Answer not a fool according to his folly, lest thou also be like unto him.   *Proverbs 26:4*

Answer a fool according to his folly, lest he be wise in his own conceit.   *Proverbs 26:5*

As a dog returneth to his vomit, so a fool returneth to his folly.   *Proverbs 26:11*

The Fool

The fear of the LORD is the beginning of knowledge: but fools despise wisdom and instruction. *Proverbs 1:7*

For the turning away of the simple shall slay them, and the prosperity of fools shall destroy them. *Proverbs 1:32*

The wise shall inherit glory: but shame shall be the promotion of fools. *Proverbs 3:35*

O ye simple, understand wisdom: and, ye fools, be ye of an understanding heart. *Proverbs 8:5*

Wisdom hath builded her house, she hath hewn out her seven pillars: She hath killed her beasts; she hath mingled her wine; she hath also furnished her table. She hath sent forth her maidens: she crieth upon the highest places of the city, Whoso is simple, let him turn in hither: as for him that wanteth understanding, she saith to him, Come, eat of my bread, and drink of the wine which I have mingled. Forsake the foolish, and live; and go in the way of understanding. *Proverbs 9:1–6*

A foolish woman is clamorous: she is simple, and knoweth nothing. For she sitteth at the door of her house, on a seat in the high places of the city, To call passengers who go right on their ways: Whoso is simple, let him turn in hither: and as for him that wanteth understanding, she saith to him, Stolen waters are sweet, and bread eaten in secret is pleasant. But he knoweth not that the dead are there; and that her guests are in the depths of hell. *Proverbs 9:13–18*

A wise son maketh a glad father: but a foolish son is the heaviness of his mother. *Proverbs 10:1*

The wise in heart will receive commandments: but a prating fool shall fall. *Proverbs 10:8*

Wise men lay up knowledge: but the mouth of the foolish is near destruction. *Proverbs 10:14*

He that hideth hatred with lying lips, and he that uttereth a slander, is a fool. *Proverbs 10:18*

The lips of the righteous feed many: but fools die for want of wisdom. *Proverbs 10:21*

It is as sport to a fool to do mischief: but a man of understanding hath wisdom. *Proverbs 10:23*

He that troubleth his own house shall inherit the wind: and the fool shall be servant to the wise of heart.

Proverbs 11:29

The way of a fool is right in his own eyes: but he that hearkeneth unto counsel is wise.
Proverbs 12:15

A fool's wrath is presently known: but a prudent man covereth shame.
Proverbs 12:16

A prudent man concealeth knowledge: but the heart of fools proclaimeth foolishness.
Proverbs 12:23

Every prudent man dealeth with knowledge: but a fool layeth open his folly.
Proverbs 13:16

The desire accomplished is sweet to the soul: but it is abomination to fools to depart from evil. *Proverbs 13:19*

He that walketh with wise men shall be wise: but a companion of fools shall be destroyed.
Proverbs 13:20

Every wise woman buildeth her house: but the foolish plucketh it down with her hands.
Proverbs 14:1

In the mouth of the foolish is a rod of pride: but the lips of the wise shall preserve them. *Proverbs 14:3*

Go from the presence of a foolish man, when thou perceivest not in him the lips of knowledge. *Proverbs 14:7*

The wisdom of the prudent is to understand his way: but the folly of fools is deceit. *Proverbs 14:8*

Fools make a mock at sin: but among the righteous there is favour. *Proverbs 14:9*

A wise man feareth, and departeth from evil: but the fool rageth, and is confident. *Proverbs 14:16*

He that is soon angry dealeth foolishly: and a man of wicked devices is hated. *Proverbs 14:17*

Wisdom resteth in the heart of him that hath understanding: but that which is in the midst of fools is made known.
Proverbs 14:33

The tongue of the wise useth knowledge aright: but the mouth of fools poureth out foolishness. *Proverbs 15:2*

A fool despiseth his father's instruction: but he that regardeth reproof is prudent. *Proverbs 15:5*

The lips of the wise disperse knowledge: but the heart of the foolish doeth not so. *Proverbs 15:7*

The heart of him that hath understanding seeketh knowledge: but the mouth of fools feedeth on foolishness. *Proverbs 15:14*

A wise son maketh a glad father: but a foolish man despiseth his mother. *Proverbs 15:20*

Excellent speech becometh not a fool: much less do lying lips a prince. *Proverbs 17:7*

A reproof entereth more into a wise man than an hundred stripes into a fool. *Proverbs 17:10*

Let a bear robbed of her whelps meet a man, rather than a fool in his folly. *Proverbs 17:12*

Wherefore is there a price in the hand of a fool to get wisdom, seeing he hath no heart to it? *Proverbs 17:16*

He that begetteth a fool doeth it to his sorrow: and the father of a fool hath no joy. *Proverbs 17:21*

Wisdom is before him that hath understanding; but the eyes of a fool are in the ends of the earth. *Proverbs 17:24*

A foolish son is a grief to his father, and bitterness to her that bare him. *Proverbs 17:25*

Even a fool, when he holdeth his peace, is counted wise: and he that shutteth his lips is esteemed a man of understanding. *Proverbs 17:28*

A fool hath no delight in understanding, but that his heart may discover itself. *Proverbs 18:2*

A fool's lips enter into contention, and his mouth calleth for strokes. *Proverbs 18:6*

A fool's mouth is his destruction, and his lips are the snare of his soul. *Proverbs 18:7*

Better is the poor that walketh in his integrity, than he that is perverse in his lips, and is a fool. *Proverbs 19:1*

The foolishness of man perverteth his way: and his heart fretteth against the LORD. *Proverbs 19:3*

Delight is not seemly for a fool; much less for a servant to have rule over princes. *Proverbs 19:10*

A foolish son is the calamity of his father: and the contentions of a wife are a continual dropping.

Proverbs 19:13

It is an honour for a man to cease from strife: but every fool will be meddling. *Proverbs 20:3*

There is treasure to be desired and oil in the dwelling of the wise; but a foolish man spendeth it up. *Proverbs 21:20*

Speak not in the ears of a fool: for he will despise the wisdom of thy words. *Proverbs 23:9*

Wisdom is too high for a fool: he openeth not his mouth in the gate. *Proverbs 24:7*

The thought of foolishness is sin: and the scorner is an abomination to men. *Proverbs 24:9*

As snow in summer, and as rain in harvest, so honour is not seemly for a fool. *Proverbs 26:1*

A whip for the horse, a bridle for the ass, and a rod for the fool's back. *Proverbs 26:3*

Answer not a fool according to his folly, lest thou also be like unto him. *Proverbs 26:4*

Answer a fool according to his folly, lest he be wise in his own conceit. *Proverbs 26:5*

He that sendeth a message by the hand of a fool cutteth off the feet, and drinketh damage. *Proverbs 26:6*

As he that bindeth a stone in a sling, so is he that giveth honour to a fool. *Proverbs 26:8*

The great God that formed all things both rewardeth the fool, and rewardeth transgressors. *Proverbs 26:10*

As a dog returneth to his vomit, so a fool returneth to his folly. *Proverbs 26:11*

Seest thou a man wise in his own conceit? there is more hope of a fool than of him. *Proverbs 26:12*

A stone is heavy, and the sand weighty; but a fool's wrath is heavier than them both. *Proverbs 27:3*

Though thou shouldest bray a fool in a mortar among wheat with a pestle, yet will not his foolishness depart from him. *Proverbs 27:22*

He that trusteth in his own heart is a fool: but whoso walketh wisely, he shall be delivered. *Proverbs 28:26*

If a wise man contendeth with a foolish man, whether he rage or laugh, there is no rest. *Proverbs 29:9*

A fool uttereth all his mind: but a wise man keepeth it in till afterwards. *Proverbs 29:11*

Seest thou a man that is hasty in his words? there is more hope of a fool than of him. *Proverbs 29:20*

Friendship

My son, if thou be surety for thy friend, if thou hast stricken thy hand with a stranger, Thou art snared with the words of thy mouth, thou art taken with the words of thy mouth. Do this now, my son, and deliver thyself, when thou art come into the hand of thy friend; go, humble thyself, and make sure thy friend. Give not sleep to thine eyes, nor slumber to thine eyelids. Deliver thyself as a roe from the hand of the hunter, and as a bird from the hand of the fowler.

Proverbs 6:1–5

The poor is hated even of his own neighbour: but the rich hath many friends. *Proverbs 14:20*

A froward man soweth strife: and a whisperer separateth chief friends. *Proverbs 16:28*

He that covereth a transgression seeketh love; but he that repeateth a matter separateth very friends. *Proverbs 17:9*

A friend loveth at all times, and a brother is born for adversity. *Proverbs 17:17*

A man void of understanding striketh hands, and becometh surety in the presence of his friend. *Proverbs 17:18*

A man that hath friends must shew himself friendly: and there is a friend that sticketh closer than a brother.

Proverbs 18:24

Wealth maketh many friends; but the poor is separated from his neighbour. *Proverbs 19:4*

Many will intreat the favour of the prince: and every man is a friend to him that giveth gifts. *Proverbs 19:6*

All the brethren of the poor do hate him: how much more do his friends go far from him? he pursueth them with words, yet they are wanting to him. *Proverbs 19:7*

He that loveth pureness of heart, for the grace of his lips the king shall be his friend. *Proverbs 22:11*

Make no friendship with an angry man; and with a furious man thou shalt not go: Lest thou learn his ways, and get a snare to thy soul. *Proverbs 22:24–25*

Faithful are the wounds of a friend; but the kisses of an enemy are deceitful. *Proverbs 27:6*

Ointment and perfume rejoice the heart: so doth the sweetness of a man's friend by hearty counsel. *Proverbs 27:9*

Thine own friend, and thy father's friend, forsake not; neither go into thy brother's house in the day of thy calamity: for better is a neighbour that is near than a brother far off.

Proverbs 27:10

He that blesseth his friend with a loud voice, rising early in the morning, it shall be counted a curse to him.

Proverbs 27:14

Iron sharpeneth iron; so a man sharpeneth the countenance of his friend.

Proverbs 27:17

As in water face answereth to face, so the heart of man to man.

Proverbs 27:19

Generosity

There is that scattereth, and yet increaseth; and there is that withholdeth more than is meet, but it tendeth to poverty.

Proverbs 11:24

The liberal soul shall be made fat: and he that watereth shall be watered also himself.   *Proverbs 11:25*

He that hath pity upon the poor lendeth unto the LORD; and that which he hath given will he pay him again.

Proverbs 19:17

The desire of the slothful killeth him; for his hands refuse to labour. He coveteth greedily all the day long: but the righteous giveth and spareth not.   *Proverbs 21:25–26*

He that hath a bountiful eye shall be blessed; for he giveth of his bread to the poor.   *Proverbs 22:9*

He that giveth unto the poor shall not lack: but he that hideth his eyes shall have many a curse.   *Proverbs 28:27*

Good

The desire of the righteous is only good: but the expectation of the wicked is wrath.   *Proverbs 11:23*

He that diligently seeketh good procureth favour: but he that seeketh mischief, it shall come unto him.
Proverbs 11:27

A man shall be satisfied with good by the fruit of his mouth: and the recompence of a man's hands shall be rendered unto him.   *Proverbs 12:14*

A man shall eat good by the fruit of his mouth: but the soul of the transgressors shall eat violence.   *Proverbs 13:2*

Evil pursueth sinners: but to the righteous good shall be repayed.   *Proverbs 13:21*

Do they not err that devise evil? but mercy and truth shall be to them that devise good.   *Proverbs 14:22*

A man hath joy by the answer of his mouth: and a word spoken in due season, how good is it!   *Proverbs 15:23*

He that handleth a matter wisely shall find good: and whoso trusteth in the LORD, happy is he.   *Proverbs 16:20*

A violent man enticeth his neighbour, and leadeth him into the way that is not good.   *Proverbs 16:29*

Whoso rewardeth evil for good, evil shall not depart from his house.   *Proverbs 17:13*

He that hath a froward heart findeth no good: and he that hath a perverse tongue falleth into mischief.
Proverbs 17:20

A merry heart doeth good like a medicine: but a broken spirit drieth the bones.   *Proverbs 17:22*

Also to punish the just is not good, nor to strike princes for equity.   *Proverbs 17:26*

It is not good to accept the person of the wicked, to overthrow the righteous in judgment.   *Proverbs 18:5*

Whoso findeth a wife findeth a good thing, and obtaineth favour of the LORD.   *Proverbs 18:22*

Also, that the soul be without knowledge, it is not good; and he that hasteth with his feet sinneth.   *Proverbs 19:2*

He that getteth wisdom loveth his own soul: he that keepeth understanding shall find good.   *Proverbs 19:8*

Most men will proclaim every one his own goodness: but a faithful man who can find?   *Proverbs 20:6*

Every purpose is established by counsel: and with good advice make war.   *Proverbs 20:18*

Divers weights are an abomination unto the LORD; and a false balance is not good.   *Proverbs 20:23*

A good name is rather to be chosen than great riches, and loving favour rather than silver and gold.   *Proverbs 22:1*

My son, eat thou honey, because it is good; and the honey-comb, which is sweet to thy taste: So shall the knowledge of wisdom be unto thy soul: when thou hast found it, then there shall be a reward, and thy expectation shall not be cut off.   *Proverbs 24:13–14*

These things also belong to the wise. It is not good to have respect of persons in judgment.   *Proverbs 24:23*

It is not good to eat much honey: so for men to search their own glory is not glory. *Proverbs 25:27*

Whoso causeth the righteous to go astray in an evil way, he shall fall himself into his own pit: but the upright shall have good things in possession. *Proverbs 28:10*

To have respect of persons is not good: for for a piece of bread that man will transgress. *Proverbs 28:21*

Who can find a virtuous woman? for her price is far above rubies. The heart of her husband doth safely trust in her, so that he shall have no need of spoil. She will do him good and not evil all the days of her life. *Proverbs 31:10-11*

Gossip

He that hideth hatred with lying lips, and he that uttereth a slander, is a fool.   *Proverbs 10:18*

A talebearer revealeth secrets: but he that is of a faithful spirit concealeth the matter.   *Proverbs 11:13*

A froward man soweth strife: and a whisperer separateth chief friends.   *Proverbs 16:28*

A wicked doer giveth heed to false lips; and a liar giveth ear to a naughty tongue.   *Proverbs 17:4*

The words of a talebearer are as wounds, and they go down into the innermost parts of the belly.   *Proverbs 18:8*

He that goeth about as a talebearer revealeth secrets: therefore meddle not with him that flattereth with his lips.
                                                     Proverbs 20:19

Go not forth hastily to strive, lest thou know not what to do in the end thereof, when thy neighbour hath put thee to shame. Debate thy cause with thy neighbour himself; and discover not a secret to another: Lest he that heareth it put thee to shame, and thine infamy turn not away.
                                                     Proverbs 25:8–10

The north wind driveth away rain: so doth an angry countenance a backbiting tongue. *Proverbs 25:23*

He that passeth by, and meddleth with strife belonging not to him, is like one that taketh a dog by the ears.

Proverbs 26:17

Where no wood is, there the fire goeth out: so where there is no talebearer, the strife ceaseth. *Proverbs 26:20*

As coals are to burning coals, and wood to fire; so is a contentious man to kindle strife. *Proverbs 26:21*

Accuse not a servant unto his master, lest he curse thee, and thou be found guilty. *Proverbs 30:10*

Guidance

Trust in the LORD with all thine heart; and lean not unto thine own understanding. In all thy ways acknowledge him, and he shall direct thy paths. Be not wise in thine own eyes: fear the LORD, and depart from evil. *Proverbs 3:5–8*

But the path of the just is as the shining light, that shineth more and more unto the perfect day. The way of the wicked is as darkness: they know not at what they stumble.
Proverbs 4:18–19

My son, keep thy father's commandment, and forsake not the law of thy mother: Bind them continually upon thine heart, and tie them about thy neck. When thou goest, it shall lead thee; when thou sleepest, it shall keep thee; and when thou awakest, it shall talk with thee. For the commandment is a lamp; and the law is light; and reproofs of instruction are the way of life. *Proverbs 6:20–23*

The integrity of the upright shall guide them: but the perverseness of transgressors shall destroy them.
Proverbs 11:3

The righteousness of the perfect shall direct his way: but the wicked shall fall by his own wickedness.
Proverbs 11:5

Without counsel purposes are disappointed: but in the multitude of counsellors they are established. *Proverbs 15:22*

A man's heart deviseth his way: but, the LORD directeth his steps. *Proverbs 16:9*

There is a way that seemeth right unto a man, but the end thereof are the ways of death. *Proverbs 16:25*

Wisdom is before him that hath understanding; but the eyes of a fool are in the ends of the earth. *Proverbs 17:24*

Also, that the soul be without knowledge, it is not good; and he that hasteth with his feet sinneth. *Proverbs 19:2*

There are many devices in a man's heart; nevertheless the counsel of the LORD, that shall stand. *Proverbs 19:21*

Man's goings are of the LORD; how can a man then understand his own way? *Proverbs 20:24*

A wicked man hardeneth his face: but as for the upright, he directeth his way. *Proverbs 21:29*

Train up a child in the way he should go: and when he is old, he will not depart from it. *Proverbs 22:6*

Hatred

The fear of the LORD is to hate evil: pride, and arrogancy, and the evil way, and the froward mouth, do I hate.

Proverbs 8:13

Now therefore hearken unto me, O ye children: for blessed are they that keep my ways. Hear instruction, and be wise, and refuse it not. Blessed is the man that heareth me, watching daily at my gates, waiting at the posts of my doors. For whoso findeth me findeth life, and shall obtain favour of the LORD. But he that sinneth against me wrongeth his own soul: all they that hate me love death.

Proverbs 8:32–36

Reprove not a scorner, lest he hate thee: rebuke a wise man, and he will love thee.

Proverbs 9:8

Hatred stirreth up strifes: but love covereth all sins.

Proverbs 10:12

He that hideth hatred with lying lips, and he that uttereth a slander, is a fool.

Proverbs 10:18

A righteous man hateth lying: but a wicked man is loathsome, and cometh to shame.

Proverbs 13:5

He that spareth his rod hateth his son: but he that loveth him chasteneth him betimes.   *Proverbs 13:24*

He that is soon angry dealeth foolishly: and a man of wicked devices is hated.   *Proverbs 14:17*

The poor is hated even of his own neighbour: but the rich hath many friends.   *Proverbs 14:20*

Correction is grievous unto him that forsaketh the way: and he that hateth reproof shall die.   *Proverbs 15:10*

Better is a dinner of herbs where love is, than a stalled ox and hatred therewith.   *Proverbs 15:17*

He that is greedy of gain troubleth his own house; but he that hateth gifts shall live.   *Proverbs 15:27*

All the brethren of the poor do hate him: how much more do his friends go far from him? he pursueth them with words, yet they are wanting to him.   *Proverbs 19:7*

Withdraw thy foot from thy neighbour's house; lest he be weary of thee, and so hate thee.   *Proverbs 25:17*

He that hateth dissembleth with his lips, and layeth up deceit within him.   *Proverbs 26:24*

Whose hatred is covered by deceit, his wickedness shall be shewed before the whole congregation.

Proverbs 26:26

A lying tongue hateth those that are afflicted by it; and a flattering mouth worketh ruin.   *Proverbs 26:28*

The prince that wanteth understanding is also a great oppressor: but he that hateth covetousness shall prolong his days.   *Proverbs 28:16*

The bloodthirsty hate the upright: but the just seek his soul.

Proverbs 29:10

Health

Be not wise in thine own eyes: fear the LORD, and depart from evil. It shall be health to thy navel, and marrow to thy bones.   *Proverbs 3:7–8*

My son, attend to my words; incline thine ear unto my sayings. Let them not depart from thine eyes; keep them in the midst of thine heart. For they are life unto those that find them, and health to all their flesh.   *Proverbs 4:20–22*

There is that speaketh like the piercings of a sword: but the tongue of the wise is health.   *Proverbs 12:18*

A wicked messenger falleth into mischief: but a faithful ambassador is health.   *Proverbs 13:17*

A sound heart is the life of the flesh: but envy the rottenness of the bones.   *Proverbs 14:30*

The light of the eyes rejoiceth the heart: and a good report maketh the bones fat.   *Proverbs 15:30*

Hearing

A wise man will hear, and will increase learning; and a man of understanding shall attain unto wise counsels.

Proverbs 1:5

My son, hear the instruction of thy father, and forsake not the law of thy mother: For they shall be an ornament of grace unto thy head, and chains about thy neck.

Proverbs 1:8–9

For the turning away of the simple shall slay them, and the prosperity of fools shall destroy them. But whoso hear-keneth unto me shall dwell safely, and shall be quiet from fear of evil.

Proverbs 1:32–33

Hear, ye children, the instruction of a father, and attend to know understanding.

Proverbs 4:1

My son, attend unto my wisdom, and bow thine ear to my understanding: That thou mayest regard discretion, and that thy lips may keep knowledge.

Proverbs 5:1–2

Doth not wisdom cry? and understanding put forth her voice? . . .Hear; for I will speak of excellent things; and the opening of my lips shall be right things.

Proverbs 8:1, 6

The way of a fool is right in his own eyes: but he that hear-keneth unto counsel is wise. *Proverbs 12:15*

A wise son heareth his father's instruction: but a scorner heareth not rebuke. *Proverbs 13:1*

The ear that heareth the reproof of life abideth among the wise. *Proverbs 15:31*

He that refuseth instruction despiseth his own soul: but he that heareth reproof getteth understanding. *Proverbs 15:32*

A wicked doer giveth heed to false lips; and a liar giveth ear to a naughty tongue. *Proverbs 17:4*

He that answereth a matter before he heareth it, it is folly and shame unto him. *Proverbs 18:13*

Hear counsel, and receive instruction, that thou mayest be wise in thy latter end. *Proverbs 19:20*

Cease, my son, to hear the instruction that causeth to err from the words of knowledge. *Proverbs 19:27*

The hearing ear, and the seeing eye, the LORD hath made even both of them. *Proverbs 20:12*

Whoso stoppeth his ears at the cry of the poor, he also shall cry himself, but shall not be heard.   *Proverbs 21:13*

A false witness shall perish: but the man that heareth speaketh constantly.   *Proverbs 21:28*

Bow down thine ear, and hear the words of the wise, and apply thine heart unto my knowledge. For it is a pleasant thing if thou keep them within thee; they shall withal be fitted in thy lips.   *Proverbs 22:17–18*

Hell

For the lips of a strange woman drop as an honeycomb, and her mouth is smoother than oil: But her end is bitter as wormwood, sharp as a twoedged sword. Her feet go down to death; her steps take hold on hell.   *Proverbs 5:3–5*

A foolish woman is clamorous: she is simple, and knoweth nothing. For she sitteth at the door of her house, on a seat in the high places of the city, To call passengers who go right on their ways: Whoso is simple, let him turn in hither: and as for him that wanteth understanding, she saith to him, Stolen waters are sweet, and bread eaten in secret is pleasant. But he knoweth not that the dead are there; and that her guests are in the depths of hell.   *Proverbs 9:13–18*

Hell and destruction are before the LORD: how much more then the hearts of the children of men?   *Proverbs 15:11*

The way of life is above to the wise, that he may depart from hell beneath.   *Proverbs 15:24*

Withhold not correction from the child: for if thou beatest him with the rod, he shall not die. Thou shalt beat him with the rod, and shalt deliver his soul from hell.

Proverbs 23:13–14

Home Life

The curse of the LORD is in the house of the wicked: but he blesseth the habitation of the just.   *Proverbs 3:33*

He that troubleth his own house shall inherit the wind: and the fool shall be servant to the wise of heart.
                                                        Proverbs 11:29

The wicked are overthrown, and are not: but the house of the righteous shall stand.   *Proverbs 12:7*

Every wise woman buildeth her house: but the foolish plucketh it down with her hands.   *Proverbs 14:1*

The house of the wicked shall be overthrown: but the tabernacle of the upright shall flourish.
                                                        Proverbs 14:11

In the fear of the LORD is strong confidence: and his children shall have a place of refuge.   *Proverbs 14:26*

In the house of the righteous is much treasure: but in the revenues of the wicked is trouble.   *Proverbs 15:6*

Better is a dinner of herbs where love is, than a stalled ox and hatred therewith. *Proverbs 15:17*

The LORD will destroy the house of the proud: but he will establish the border of the widow. *Proverbs 15:25*

He that is greedy of gain troubleth his own house; but he that hateth gifts shall live. *Proverbs 15:27*

Better is a dry morsel, and quietness therewith, than an house full of sacrifices with strife. *Proverbs 17:1*

Whoso rewardeth evil for good, evil shall not depart from his house. *Proverbs 17:13*

It is better to dwell in a corner of the housetop, than with a brawling woman in a wide house. *Proverbs 21:9*

The righteous man wisely considereth the house of the wicked: but God overthroweth the wicked for their wickedness. *Proverbs 21:12*

There is treasure to be desired and oil in the dwelling of the wise; but a foolish man spendeth it up. *Proverbs 21:20*

Honor & Glory

Honour the LORD with thy substance, and with the first-fruits of all thine increase: So shall thy barns be filled with plenty, and thy presses shall burst out with new wine.

Proverbs 3:9–10

Happy is the man that findeth wisdom, and the man that getteth understanding. For the merchandise of it is better than the merchandise of silver, and the gain thereof than fine gold. She is more precious than rubies: and all the things thou canst desire are not to be compared unto her. Length of days is in her right hand; and in her left hand riches and honour

Proverbs 3:13–16

The wise shall inherit glory: but shame shall be the promotion of fools.

Proverbs 3:35

Wisdom is the principal thing; therefore get wisdom: and with all thy getting get understanding. Exalt her, and she shall promote thee: she shall bring thee to honour, when thou dost embrace her. She shall give to thine head an ornament of grace: a crown of glory shall she deliver to thee.

Proverbs 4:7–9

For the lips of a strange woman drop as an honeycomb, and her mouth is smoother than oil. . . Remove thy way far from her, and come not nigh the door of her house: Lest thou give thine honour unto others, and thy years unto the cruel.
Proverbs 5:3,8–9

But whoso committeth adultery with a woman lacketh understanding: he that doeth it destroyeth his own soul. A wound and dishonour shall he get; and his reproach shall not be wiped away.
Proverbs 6:32–33

A gracious woman retaineth honour: and strong men retain riches.
Proverbs 11:16

He that is despised, and hath a servant, is better than he that honoureth himself, and lacketh bread.
Proverbs 12:9

Poverty and shame shall be to him that refuseth instruction: but he that regardeth reproof shall be honoured.
Proverbs 13:18

In the multitude of people is the king's honour: but in the want of people is the destruction of the prince.
Proverbs 14:28

The fear of the LORD is the instruction of wisdom; and before honour is humility.
Proverbs 15:33

The hoary head is a crown of glory, if it be found in the way of righteousness.   *Proverbs 16:31*

Children's children are the crown of old men; and the glory of children are their fathers.   *Proverbs 17:6*

Before destruction the heart of man is haughty, and before honour is humility.   *Proverbs 18:12*

The discretion of a man deferreth his anger; and it is his glory to pass over a transgression.   *Proverbs 19:11*

It is an honour for a man to cease from strife: but every fool will be meddling.   *Proverbs 20:3*

The glory of young men is their strength: and the beauty of old men is the gray head.   *Proverbs 20:29*

He that followeth after righteousness and mercy findeth life, righteousness, and honour.   *Proverbs 21:21*

By humility and the fear of the LORD are riches, and honour, and life.   *Proverbs 22:4*

It is the glory of God to conceal a thing: but the honour of kings is to search out a matter.   *Proverbs 25:2*

Put not forth thyself in the presence of the king, and stand not in the place of great men: For better it is that it be said unto thee, Come up hither; than that thou shouldest be put lower in the presence of the prince whom thine eyes have seen.   *Proverbs 25:6*

It is not good to eat much honey: so for men to search their own glory is not glory.   *Proverbs 25:27*

As snow in summer, and as rain in harvest, so honour is not seemly for a fool.   *Proverbs 26:1*

As he that bindeth a stone in a sling, so is he that giveth honour to a fool.   *Proverbs 26:8*

Let another man praise thee, and not thine own mouth; a stranger, and not thine own lips.   *Proverbs 27:2*

Whoso keepeth the fig tree shall eat the fruit thereof: so he that waiteth on his master shall be honoured.
                                                        Proverbs 27:18

A man's pride shall bring him low: but honour shall uphold the humble in spirit.   *Proverbs 29:23*

Hope

The hope of the righteous shall be gladness: but the expectation of the wicked shall perish. *Proverbs 10:28*

When a wicked man dieth, his expectation shall perish: and the hope of unjust men perisheth. *Proverbs 11:7*

Hope deferred maketh the heart sick: but when the desire cometh, it is a tree of life. *Proverbs 13:12*

The wicked is driven away in his wickedness: but the righteous hath hope in his death. *Proverbs 14:32*

Chasten thy son while there is hope, and let not thy soul spare for his crying. *Proverbs 19:18*

Seest thou a man wise in his own conceit? there is more hope of a fool than of him. *Proverbs 26:12*

Seest thou a man hasty in his words? there is mor hope of a fool than of him. *Proverbs 29:20*

Humility

Surely he scorneth the scorners: but he giveth grace unto the lowly.
Proverbs 3:34

When pride cometh, then cometh shame: but with the lowly is wisdom.
Proverbs 11:2

The fear of the LORD is the instruction of wisdom; and before honour is humility.
Proverbs 15:33

Better it is to be of an humble spirit with the lowly, than to divide the spoil with the proud.
Proverbs 16:19

Before destruction the heart of man is haughty, and before honour is humility.
Proverbs 18:12

By humility and the fear of the LORD are riches, and honour, and life.
Proverbs 22:4

A man's pride shall bring him low: but honour shall uphold the humble in spirit.
Proverbs 29:23

Iniquity

His own iniquities shall take the wicked himself, and he shall be holden with the cords of his sins. He shall die without instruction; and in the greatness of his folly he shall go astray.   *Proverbs 5:22,23*

The way of the LORD is strength to the upright: but destruction shall be to the workers of iniquity.   *Proverbs 10:29*

By mercy and truth iniquity is purged: and by the fear of the LORD men depart from evil.   *Proverbs 16:6*

An ungodly witness scorneth judgment: and the mouth of the wicked devoureth iniquity.   *Proverbs 19:28*

It is joy to the just to do judgment: but destruction shall be to the workers of iniquity.   *Proverbs 21:15*

He that soweth iniquity shall reap vanity: and the rod of his anger shall fail.   *Proverbs 22:8*

Instruction

The fear of the LORD is the beginning of knowledge: but fools despise wisdom and instruction.   *Proverbs 1:7*

My son, hear the instruction of thy father, and forsake not the law of thy mother: For they shall be an ornament of grace unto thy head, and chains about thy neck.
Proverbs 1:8–9

My son, forget not my law; but let thine heart keep my commandments: For length of days, and long life, and peace, shall they add to thee.   *Proverbs 3:1–2*

Hear, ye children, the instruction of a father, and attend to know understanding. For I give you good doctrine, forsake ye not my law. For I was my father's son, tender and only beloved in the sight of my mother. He taught me also, and said unto me, Let thine heart retain my words: keep my commandments, and live.   *Proverbs 4:1–4*

Take fast hold of instruction; let her not go: keep her; for she is thy life.   *Proverbs 4:13*

My son, attend to my words; incline thine ear unto my sayings. Let them not depart from thine eyes; keep them in the midst of thine heart. For they are life unto those that find them, and health to all their flesh.   *Proverbs 4:20–22*

My son, attend unto my wisdom, and bow thine ear to my understanding: That thou mayest regard discretion, and that thy lips may keep knowledge. . .thou mourn at the last, when thy flesh and thy body are consumed, And say, How have I hated instruction, and my heart despised reproof; And have not obeyed the voice of my teachers, nor inclined mine ear to them that instructed me! I was almost in all evil in the midst of the congregation and assembly.

Proverbs 5:1, 2, 9, 11, 14

His own iniquities shall take the wicked himself, and he shall be holden with the cords of his sins. He shall die without instruction; and in the greatness of his folly he shall go astray.   *Proverbs 5:22–23*

For the commandment is a lamp; and the law is light; and reproofs of instruction are the way of life.   *Proverbs 6:23*

My son, keep my words, and lay up my commandments with thee. Keep my commandments, and live; and my law as the apple of thine eye.   *Proverbs 7:1–52*

Doth not wisdom cry? and understanding put forth her voice? . . .Unto you, O men, I call; and my voice is to the sons of man. . .Receive my instruction, and not silver; and knowledge rather than choice gold. For wisdom is better than rubies; and all the things that may be desired are not to be compared to it.   *Proverbs 8:1,4,10–11*

Now therefore hearken unto me, O ye children: for blessed are they that keep my ways. Hear instruction, and be wise, and refuse it not. *Proverbs 8:32–33*

Give instruction to a wise man, and he will be yet wiser: teach a just man, and he will increase in learning.
Proverbs 9:9

He is in the way of life that keepeth instruction: but he that refuseth reproof erreth. *Proverbs 10:17*

Whoso loveth instruction loveth knowledge: but he that hateth reproof is brutish. *Proverbs 12:1*

A wise son heareth his father's instruction: but a scorner heareth not rebuke. *Proverbs 13:1*

The law of the wise is a fountain of life, to depart from the snares of death. *Proverbs 13:14*

Poverty and shame shall be to him that refuseth instruction: but he that regardeth reproof shall be honoured.
Proverbs 13:18

A fool despiseth his father's instruction: but he that regardeth reproof is prudent. *Proverbs 15:5*

He that refuseth instruction despiseth his own soul: but he that heareth reproof getteth understanding.

Proverbs 15:32

The fear of the LORD is the instruction of wisdom; and before honour is humility.   *Proverbs 15:33*

Understanding is a wellspring of life unto him that hath it: but the instruction of fools is folly.   *Proverbs 16:22*

He that getteth wisdom loveth his own soul: he that keepeth understanding shall find good.   *Proverbs 19:8*

He that keepeth the commandment keepeth his own soul; but he that despiseth his ways shall die.   *Proverbs 19:16*

Hear counsel, and receive instruction, that thou mayest be wise in thy latter end.   *Proverbs 19:20*

Cease, my son, to hear the instruction that causeth to err from the words of knowledge.   *Proverbs 19:27*

When the scorner is punished, the simple is made wise: and when the wise is instructed, he receiveth knowledge.

Proverbs 21:11

Apply thine heart unto instruction, and thine ears to the words of knowledge.   *Proverbs 23:12*

Buy the truth, and sell it not; also wisdom, and instruction, and understanding.   *Proverbs 23:23*

They that forsake the law praise the wicked: but such as keep the law contend with them.   *Proverbs 28:4*

Whoso keepeth the law is a wise son: but he that is a companion of riotous men shameth his father.

Proverbs 28:7

He that turneth away his ear from hearing the law, even his prayer shall be abomination.   *Proverbs 28:9*

Where there is no vision, the people perish: but he that keepeth the law, happy is he.   *Proverbs 29:18*

Integrity

For the LORD giveth wisdom: out of his mouth cometh knowledge and understanding. He layeth up sound wisdom for the righteous: he is a buckler to them that walk uprightly.

Proverbs 2:6–7

For the upright shall dwell in the land, and the perfect shall remain in it. But the wicked shall be cut off from the earth, and the transgressors shall be rooted out of it.

Proverbs 2:21–22

He that walketh uprightly walketh surely: but he that perverteth his ways shall be known. *Proverbs 10:9*

The way of the LORD is strength to the upright: but destruction shall be to the workers of iniquity. *Proverbs 10:29*

The integrity of the upright shall guide them: but the perverseness of transgressors shall destroy them.

Proverbs 11:3

The righteousness of the perfect shall direct his way: but the wicked shall fall by his own wickedness.

Proverbs 11:5

The righteousness of the upright shall deliver them: but transgressors shall be taken in their own naughtiness.

Proverbs 11:6

By the blessing of the upright the city is exalted: but it is overthrown by the mouth of the wicked.   *Proverbs 11:11*

They that are of a froward heart are abomination to the LORD: but such as are upright in their way are his delight.

Proverbs 11:20

The words of the wicked are to lie in wait for blood: but the mouth of the upright shall deliver them.   *Proverbs 12:6*

Righteousness keepeth him that is upright in the way: but wickedness overthroweth the sinner.   *Proverbs 13:6*

He that walketh in his uprightness feareth the LORD: but he that is perverse in his ways despiseth him.   *Proverbs 14:2*

The house of the wicked shall be overthrown: but the tabernacle of the upright shall flourish.   *Proverbs 14:11*

The sacrifice of the wicked is an abomination to the LORD: but the prayer of the upright is his delight.

Proverbs 15:8

Folly is joy to him that is destitute of wisdom: but a man of understanding walketh uprightly. *Proverbs 15:21*

The highway of the upright is to depart from evil: he that keepeth his way preserveth his soul. *Proverbs 16:17*

Better is the poor that walketh in his integrity, than he that is perverse in his lips, and is a fool. *Proverbs 19:1*

The just man walketh in his integrity: his children are blessed after him. *Proverbs 20:7*

Even a child is known by his doings, whether his work be pure, and whether it be right. *Proverbs 20:11*

The way of man is froward and strange: but as for the pure, his work is right. *Proverbs 21:8*

The wicked shall be a ransom for the righteous, and the transgressor for the upright. *Proverbs 21:18*

A wicked man hardeneth his face: but as for the upright, he directeth his way. *Proverbs 21:29*

Better is the poor that walketh in his uprightness, than he that is perverse in his ways, though he be rich. *Proverbs 28:6*

Whoso causeth the righteous to go astray in an evil way, he shall fall himself into his own pit: but the upright shall have good things in possession. *Proverbs 28:10*

Whoso walketh uprightly shall be saved: but he that is perverse in his ways shall fall at once. *Proverbs 28:18*

The bloodthirsty hate the upright: but the just seek his soul. *Proverbs 29:10*

An unjust man is an abomination to the just: and he that is upright in the way is abomination to the wicked. *Proverbs 29:27*

Joy & Gladness

Let thy fountain be blessed: and rejoice with the wife of thy youth.
Proverbs 5:18

A wise son maketh a glad father: but a foolish son is the heaviness of his mother.
Proverbs 10:1

The hope of the righteous shall be gladness: but the expectation of the wicked shall perish.
Proverbs 10:28

When it goeth well with the righteous, the city rejoiceth: and when the wicked perish, there is shouting.
Proverbs 11:10

Deceit is in the heart of them that imagine evil: but to the counsellors of peace is joy.
Proverbs 12:20

Heaviness in the heart of man maketh it stoop: but a good word maketh it glad.
Proverbs 12:25

The light of the righteous rejoiceth: but the lamp of the wicked shall be put out.
Proverbs 13:9

The heart knoweth his own bitterness; and a stranger doth not intermeddle with his joy. *Proverbs 14:10*

A wise son maketh a glad father: but a foolish man despiseth his mother. *Proverbs 15:20*

Folly is joy to him that is destitute of wisdom: but a man of understanding walketh uprightly. *Proverbs 15:21*

A man hath joy by the answer of his mouth: and a word spoken in due season, how good is it! *Proverbs 15:23*

The light of the eyes rejoiceth the heart: and a good report maketh the bones fat. *Proverbs 15:30*

Whoso mocketh the poor reproacheth his Maker: and he that is glad at calamities shall not be unpunished.
Proverbs 17:5

He that begetteth a fool doeth it to his sorrow: and the father of a fool hath no joy. *Proverbs 17:21*

It is joy to the just to do judgment: but destruction shall be to the workers of iniquity. *Proverbs 21:15*

My son, if thine heart be wise, my heart shall rejoice, even mine. Yea, my reins shall rejoice, when thy lips speak right things. *Proverbs 23:15–16*

The father of the righteous shall greatly rejoice: and he that begetteth a wise child shall have joy of him. Thy father and thy mother shall be glad, and she that bare thee shall rejoice. *Proverbs 23:24–25*

Rejoice not when thine enemy falleth, and let not thine heart be glad when he stumbleth: Lest the LORD see it, and it displease him, and he turn away his wrath from him. *Proverbs 24:17–18*

Ointment and perfume rejoice the heart: so doth the sweetness of a man's friend by hearty counsel. *Proverbs 27:9*

My son, be wise, and make my heart glad, that I may answer him that reproacheth me. *Proverbs 27:11*

When righteous men do rejoice, there is great glory: but when the wicked rise, a man is hidden. *Proverbs 28:12*

When the righteous are in authority, the people rejoice: but when the wicked beareth rule, the people mourn. *Proverbs 29:2*

Judgment

Treasures of wickedness profit nothing: but righteousness delivereth from death.   *Proverbs 10:2*

The fear of the wicked, it shall come upon him: but the desire of the righteous shall be granted. As the whirlwind passeth, so is the wicked no more: but the righteous is an everlasting foundation.   *Proverbs 10:24–25*

The way of the LORD is strength to the upright: but destruction shall be to the workers of iniquity.   *Proverbs 10:29*

The righteous shall never be removed: but the wicked shall not inhabit the earth.   *Proverbs 10:30*

Riches profit not in the day of wrath: but righteousness delivereth from death.   *Proverbs 11:4*

Though hand join in hand, the wicked shall not be unpunished: but the seed of the righteous shall be delivered.
                    Proverbs 11:21

The desire of the righteous is only good: but the expectation of the wicked is wrath.   *Proverbs 11:23*

A good man obtaineth favour of the LORD: but a man of wicked devices will he condemn.   *Proverbs 12:2*

Much food is in the tillage of the poor: but there is that is destroyed for want of judgment.   *Proverbs 13:23*

All the ways of a man are clean in his own eyes; but the LORD weigheth the spirits.   *Proverbs 16:2*

The LORD hath made all things for himself: yea, even the wicked for the day of evil.   *Proverbs 16:4*

Every one that is proud in heart is an abomination to the LORD: though hand join in hand, he shall not be unpunished.
           Proverbs 16:5

The fining pot is for silver, and the furnace for gold: but the LORD trieth the hearts.   *Proverbs 17:3*

Whoso mocketh the poor reproacheth his Maker: and he that is glad at calamities shall not be unpunished.
           Proverbs 17:5

A wicked man taketh a gift out of the bosom to pervert the ways of judgment.   *Proverbs 17:23*

Also, to punish the just is not good, nor to strike princes for equity.   *Proverbs 17:26*

It is not good to accept the person of the wicked, to overthrow the righteous in judgment.   *Proverbs 18:5*

He that is first in his own cause seemeth just; but his neighbour cometh and searcheth him.   *Proverbs 18:17*

A false witness shall not be unpunished, and he that speaketh lies shall not escape.   *Proverbs 19:5*

A false witness shall not be unpunished, and he that speaketh lies shall perish.   *Proverbs 19:9*

An ungodly witness scorneth judgment: and the mouth of the wicked devoureth iniquity.   *Proverbs 19:28*

A king that sitteth in the throne of judgment scattereth away all evil with his eyes.   *Proverbs 20:8*

To do justice and judgment is more acceptable to the LORD than sacrifice.   *Proverbs 21:3*

The robbery of the wicked shall destroy them; because they refuse to do judgment.   *Proverbs 21:7*

It is joy to the just to do judgment: but destruction shall be to the workers of iniquity.   *Proverbs 21:15*

A false witness shall perish: but the man that heareth speaketh constantly.   *Proverbs 21:28*

The mouth of strange women is a deep pit: he that is abhorred of the LORD shall fall therein.   *Proverbs 22:14*

These things also belong to the wise. It is not good to have respect of persons in judgment.   *Proverbs 24:23*

He that saith unto the wicked, Thou art righteous; him shall the people curse, nations shall abhor him: But to them that rebuke him shall be delight, and a good blessing shall come upon them.   *Proverbs 24:24–25*

The great God that formed all things both rewardeth the fool, and rewardeth transgressors.   *Proverbs 26:10*

They that forsake the law praise the wicked: but such as keep the law contend with them.   *Proverbs 28:4*

Evil men understand not judgment: but they that seek the LORD understand all things.   *Proverbs 28:5*

A man that doeth violence to the blood of any person shall flee to the pit; let no man stay him.   _Proverbs 28:17_

The king by judgment establisheth the land: but he that receiveth gifts overthroweth it.   _Proverbs 29:4_

Scornful men bring a city into a snare: but wise men turn away wrath.   _Proverbs 29:8_

Many seek the ruler's favour; but every man's judgment cometh from the LORD.   _Proverbs 29:26_

It is not for kings, O Lemuel, it is not for kings to drink wine; nor for princes strong drink: Lest they drink, and forget the law, and pervert the judgment of any of the afflicted.
               Proverbs 31:4–5

Kings & Rulers

I wisdom dwell with prudence, and find out knowledge of witty inventions. The fear of the LORD is to hate evil: pride, and arrogancy, and the evil way, and the froward mouth, do I hate. Counsel is mine, and sound wisdom: I am understanding; I have strength. By me kings reign, and princes decree justice. By me princes rule, and nobles, even all the judges of the earth. *Proverbs 8:12–16*

The hand of the diligent shall bear rule: but the slothful shall be under tribute. *Proverbs 12:24*

In the multitude of people is the king's honour: but in the want of people is the destruction of the prince.
Proverbs 14:28

The king's favour is toward a wise servant: but his wrath is against him that causeth shame. *Proverbs 14:35*

A divine sentence is in the lips of the king: his mouth transgresseth not in judgment. *Proverbs 16:10*

It is an abomination to kings to commit wickedness: for the throne is established by righteousness. *Proverbs 16:12*

Righteous lips are the delight of kings; and they love him that speaketh right. *Proverbs 16:13*

The wrath of a king is as messengers of death: but a wise man will pacify it. *Proverbs 16:14*

In the light of the king's countenance is life; and his favour is as a cloud of the latter rain. *Proverbs 16:15*

He that is slow to anger is better than the mighty; and he that ruleth his spirit than he that taketh a city. *Proverbs 16:32*

A wise servant shall have rule over a son that causeth shame, and shall have part of the inheritance among the brethren. *Proverbs 17:2*

Delight is not seemly for a fool; much less for a servant to have rule over princes. *Proverbs 19:10*

The king's wrath is as the roaring of a lion; but his favour is as dew upon the grass. *Proverbs 19:12*

The fear of a king is as the roaring of a lion: whoso provoketh him to anger sinneth against his own soul. *Proverbs 20:2*

A king that sitteth in the throne of judgment scattereth away all evil with his eyes.   *Proverbs 20:8*

A wise king scattereth the wicked, and bringeth the wheel over them.   *Proverbs 20:26*

Mercy and truth preserve the king: and his throne is upholden by mercy.   *Proverbs 20:28*

The king's heart is in the hand of the LORD, as the rivers of water: he turneth it whithersoever he will.   *Proverbs 21:1*

The rich ruleth over the poor, and the borrower is servant to the lender.   *Proverbs 22:7*

He that loveth pureness of heart, for the grace of his lips the king shall be his friend.   *Proverbs 22:11*

Seest thou a man diligent in his business? he shall stand before kings; he shall not stand before mean men.

Proverbs 22:29

When thou sittest to eat with a ruler, consider diligently what is before thee: And put a knife to thy throat, if thou be a man given to appetite. Be not desirous of his dainties: for they are deceitful meat.   *Proverbs 23:1–3*

My son, fear thou the LORD and the king: and meddle not with them that are given to change: _Proverbs 24:21_

It is the glory of God to conceal a thing: but the honour of kings is to search out a matter.   _Proverbs 25:2_

The heaven for height, and the earth for depth, and the heart of kings is unsearchable.   _Proverbs 25:3_

Take away the dross from the silver, and there shall come forth a vessel for the finer. Take away the wicked from before the king, and his throne shall be established in right-eousness.   _Proverbs 25:4–5_

Put not forth thyself in the presence of the king, and stand not in the place of great men: For better it is that it be said unto thee, Come up hither; than that thou shouldest be put lower in the presence of the prince whom thine eyes have seen.   _Proverbs 25:6–7_

Be thou diligent to know the state of thy flocks, and look well to thy herds. For riches are not for ever: and doth the crown endure to every generation?   _Proverbs 27:23–24_

As a roaring lion, and a ranging bear; so is a wicked ruler over the poor people.   _Proverbs 28:15_

When the righteous are in authority, the people rejoice: but when the wicked beareth rule, the people mourn.

Proverbs 29:2

The king by judgment establisheth the land: but he that receiveth gifts overthroweth it.   *Proverbs 29:4*

If a ruler hearken to lies, all his servants are wicked.

Proverbs 29:12

The king that faithfully judgeth the poor, his throne shall be established for ever.   *Proverbs 29:14*

Many seek the ruler's favour; but every man's judgment cometh from the LORD.   *Proverbs 29:26*

There be three things which go well, yea, four are comely in going: A lion which is strongest among beasts, and turneth not away for any; A greyhound; an he goat also; and a king, against whom there is no rising up.   *Proverbs 30:29–31*

Give not thy strength unto women, nor thy ways to that which destroyeth kings. It is not for kings, O Lemuel, it is not for kings to drink wine; nor for princes strong drink: Lest they drink, and forget the law, and pervert the judgment of any of the afflicted.   *Proverbs 31:3–5*

Knowledge

The fear of the LORD is the beginning of knowledge: but fools despise wisdom and instruction.   *Proverbs 1:7*

For the LORD giveth wisdom; out of his mouth cometh knowledge and understanding.   *Proverbs 2:6*

The LORD by wisdom hath founded the earth; by understanding hath he established the heavens. By his knowledge the depths are broken up, and the clouds drop down the dew.   *Proverbs 3:19–20*

My son, attend unto my wisdom, and bow thine ear to my understanding: That thou mayest regard discretion, and that thy lips may keep knowledge.   *Proverbs 5:1–2*

Receive my instruction, and not silver; and knowledge rather than choice gold. For wisdom is better than rubies; and all the things that may be desired are not to be compared to it. I wisdom dwell with prudence, and find out knowledge of witty inventions.   *Proverbs 8:10–12*

The fear of the LORD is the beginning of wisdom: and the knowledge of the holy is understanding. For by me thy days shall be multiplied, and the years of thy life shall be increased.   *Proverbs 9:10–11*

Wise men lay up knowledge: but the mouth of the foolish is near destruction. *Proverbs 10:14*

An hypocrite with his mouth destroyeth his neighbour: but through knowledge shall the just be delivered.

Proverbs 11:9

Whoso loveth instruction loveth knowledge: but he that hateth reproof is brutish. *Proverbs 12:1*

A prudent man concealeth knowledge: but the heart of fools proclaimeth foolishness. *Proverbs 12:23*

Every prudent man dealeth with knowledge: but a fool layeth open his folly. *Proverbs 13:16*

A scorner seeketh wisdom, and findeth it not: but knowledge is easy unto him that understandeth. *Proverbs 14:6*

Go from the presence of a foolish man, when thou perceivest not in him the lips of knowledge. *Proverbs 14:7*

The simple inherit folly: but the prudent are crowned with knowledge. *Proverbs 14:18*

The tongue of the wise useth knowledge aright: but the mouth of fools poureth out foolishness. *Proverbs 15:2*

The lips of the wise disperse knowledge: but the heart of the foolish doeth not so.   *Proverbs 15:7*

The heart of him that hath understanding seeketh knowledge: but the mouth of fools feedeth on foolishness.
Proverbs 15:14

He that hath knowledge spareth his words: and a man of understanding is of an excellent spirit.   *Proverbs 17:27*

The heart of the prudent getteth knowledge; and the ear of the wise seeketh knowledge.   *Proverbs 18:15*

Also, that the soul be without knowledge, it is not good; and he that hasteth with his feet sinneth.   *Proverbs 19:2*

Smite a scorner, and the simple will beware: and reprove one that hath understanding, and he will understand knowledge.
Proverbs 19:25

Cease, my son, to hear the instruction that causeth to err from the words of knowledge.   *Proverbs 19:27*

There is gold, and a multitude of rubies: but the lips of knowledge are a precious jewel.   *Proverbs 20:15*

When the scorner is punished, the simple is made wise: and when the wise is instructed, he receiveth knowledge.

Proverbs 21:11

The eyes of the LORD preserve knowledge, and he over-throweth the words of the transgressor.   *Proverbs 22:12*

Bow down thine ear, and hear the words of the wise, and apply thine heart unto my knowledge. For it is a pleasant thing if thou keep them within thee; they shall withal be fitted in thy lips.   *Proverbs 22:17–18*

That thy trust may be in the LORD, I have made known to thee this day, even to thee. Have not I written to thee excellent things in counsels and knowledge, That I might make thee know the certainty of the words of truth; that thou mightest answer the words of truth to them that send unto thee?   *Proverbs 22:19–21*

Apply thine heart unto instruction, and thine ears to the words of knowledge.   *Proverbs 23:12*

Through wisdom is an house builded; and by understanding it is established: And by knowledge shall the chambers be filled with all precious and pleasant riches.   *Proverbs 24:3–4*

A wise man is strong; yea, a man of knowledge increaseth strength.   *Proverbs 24:5*

Lending

He that hath pity upon the poor lendeth unto the LORD; and that which he hath given will he pay him again.

Proverbs 19:17

The rich ruleth over the poor, and the borrower is servant to the lender. *Proverbs 22:7*

He that by usury and unjust gain increaseth his substance, he shall gather it for him that will pity the poor.

Proverbs 28:8

Life

My son, let not them depart from thine eyes: keep sound wisdom and discretion: So shall they be life unto thy soul, and grace to thy neck.   *Proverbs 3:21–22*

Take fast hold of instruction; let her not go: keep her; for she is thy life.   *Proverbs 4:13*

My son, attend to my words; incline thine ear unto my sayings. Let them not depart from thine eyes; keep them in the midst of thine heart. For they are life unto those that find them, and health to all their flesh.   *Proverbs 4:20–22*

Keep thy heart with all diligence; for out of it are the issues of life.   *Proverbs 4:23*

For the commandment is a lamp; and the law is light; and reproofs of instruction are the way of life   *Proverbs 6:23*

My son, keep my words, and lay up my commandments with thee. Keep my commandments, and live; and my law as the apple of thine eye.   *Proverbs 7:1–2*

Now therefore hearken unto me, O ye children: for blessed are they that keep my ways. . .For whoso findeth me findeth life, and shall obtain favour of the LORD. But he that sinneth against me wrongeth his own soul: all they that hate me love death.   *Proverbs 8:32, 35, 36*

Forsake the foolish, and live; and go in the way of understanding.   *Proverbs 9:6*

The mouth of a righteous man is a well of life: but violence covereth the mouth of the wicked.   *Proverbs 10:11*

The labour of the righteous tendeth to life: the fruit of the wicked to sin.   *Proverbs 10:16*

He is in the way of life that keepeth instruction: but he that refuseth reproof erreth.   *Proverbs 10:17*

As righteousness tendeth to life: so he that pursueth evil pursueth it to his own death.   *Proverbs 11:19*

The fruit of the righteous is a tree of life; and he that winneth souls is wise.   *Proverbs 11:30*

In the way of righteousness is life; and in the pathway thereof there is no death.   *Proverbs 12:28*

He that keepeth his mouth keepeth his life: but he that openeth wide his lips shall have destruction.

Proverbs 13:3

Hope deferred maketh the heart sick: but when the desire cometh, it is a tree of life. *Proverbs 13:12*

The law of the wise is a fountain of life, to depart from the snares of death. *Proverbs 13:14*

The fear of the LORD is a fountain of life, to depart from the snares of death. *Proverbs 14:27*

A sound heart is the life of the flesh: but envy the rottenness of the bones. *Proverbs 14:30*

A wholesome tongue is a tree of life: but perverseness therein is a breach in the spirit. *Proverbs 15:4*

The way of life is above to the wise, that he may depart from hell beneath. *Proverbs 15:24*

He that is greedy of gain troubleth his own house; but he that hateth gifts shall live. *Proverbs 15:27*

The ear that heareth the reproof of life abideth among the wise.   *Proverbs 15:31*

In the light of the king's countenance is life; and his favour is as a cloud of the latter rain.   *Proverbs 16:15*

Understanding is a wellspring of life unto him that hath it: but the instruction of fools is folly.   *Proverbs 16:22*

Death and life are in the power of the tongue: and they that love it shall eat the fruit thereof.   *Proverbs 18:21*

Love

My son, despise not the chastening of the LORD; neither be weary of his correction: For whom the LORD loveth he correcteth; even as a father the son in whom he delighteth.

Proverbs 3:11–12

Get wisdom, get understanding: forget it not; neither decline from the words of my mouth. Forsake her not, and she shall preserve thee: love her, and she shall keep thee.

Proverbs 4:5–6

Let thy fountain be blessed: and rejoice with the wife of thy youth. Let her be as the loving hind and pleasant roe; let her breasts satisfy thee at all times; and be thou ravished always with her love.

Proverbs 5:18–19

Doth not wisdom cry? and understanding put forth her voice? . . .Unto you, O men, I call; and my voice is to the sons of man. . .I love them that love me; and those that seek me early shall find me. . .I lead in the way of righteousness, in the midst of the paths of judgment: That I may cause those that love me to inherit substance; and I will fill their treasures.

Proverbs 8:1, 4, 17, 20–21

Reprove not a scorner, lest he hate thee: rebuke a wise man, and he will love thee.

Proverbs 9:8

Hatred stirreth up strifes: but love covereth all sins.
Proverbs 10:12

The way of the wicked is an abomination unto the LORD: but he loveth him that followeth after righteousness.
Proverbs 15:9

A scorner loveth not one that reproveth him: neither will he go unto the wise. *Proverbs 15:12*

Better is a dinner of herbs where love is, than a stalled ox and hatred therewith. *Proverbs 15:17*

Righteous lips are the delight of kings; and they love him that speaketh right. *Proverbs 16:13*

He that covereth a transgression seeketh love; but he that repeateth a matter separateth very friends.
Proverbs 17:9

A friend loveth at all times, and a brother is born for adversity. *Proverbs 17:17*

He loveth transgression that loveth strife: and he that exalteth his gate seeketh destruction. *Proverbs 17:19*

Death and life are in the power of the tongue: and they that love it shall eat the fruit thereof. *Proverbs 18:21*

Love not sleep, lest thou come to poverty; open thine eyes, and thou shalt be satisfied with bread.

Proverbs 20:13

He that loveth pleasure shall be a poor man: he that loveth wine and oil shall not be rich. *Proverbs 21:17*

He that loveth pureness of heart, for the grace of his lips the king shall be his friend. *Proverbs 22:11*

Open rebuke is better than secret love. *Proverbs 27:5*

Whoso loveth wisdom rejoiceth his father: but he that keepeth company with harlots spendeth his substance.

Proverbs 29:3

Lying

These six things doth the LORD hate: yea, seven are an abomination unto him: A proud look, a lying tongue, and hands that shed innocent blood, An heart that deviseth wicked imaginations, feet that be swift in running to mischief. A false witness that speaketh lies, and he that soweth discord among brethren.   *Proverbs 6:16–19*

He that hideth hatred with lying lips, and he that uttereth a slander, is a fool.   *Proverbs 10:18*

He that speaketh truth sheweth forth righteousness: but a false witness deceit.   *Proverbs 12:17*

The lip of truth shall be established for ever: but a lying tongue is but for a moment.   *Proverbs 12:19*

Lying lips are abomination to the LORD: but they that deal truly are his delight.   *Proverbs 12:22*

A righteous man hateth lying: but a wicked man is loathsome, and cometh to shame.   *Proverbs 13:5*

A faithful witness will not lie: but a false witness will utter lies.   *Proverbs 14:5*

A true witness delivereth souls: but a deceitful witness speaketh lies.   *Proverbs 14:25*

A wicked doer giveth heed to false lips; and a liar giveth ear to a naughty tongue.   *Proverbs 17:4*

Excellent speech becometh not a fool: much less do lying lips a prince.   *Proverbs 17:7*

A false witness shall not be unpunished, and he that speaketh lies shall not escape.   *Proverbs 19:5*

A false witness shall not be unpunished, and he that speaketh lies shall perish.   *Proverbs 19:9*

An ungodly witness scorneth judgment: and the mouth of the wicked devoureth iniquity.   *Proverbs 19:28*

The getting of treasures by a lying tongue is a vanity tossed to and fro of them that seek death.   *Proverbs 21:6*

A false witness shall perish: but the man that heareth speaketh constantly.   *Proverbs 21:28*

Be not a witness against thy neighbour without cause; and
deceive not with thy lips. Say not, I will do also to him as
he hath done to me: I will render to the man according to
his work.   *Proverbs 24:28–29*

A man that beareth false witness against his neighbour is a
maul, and a sword, and a sharp arrow.

Proverbs 25:18

A lying tongue hateth those that are afflicted by it; and a
flattering mouth worketh ruin.   *Proverbs 26:28*

If a ruler hearken to lies, all his servants are wicked.

Proverbs 29:12

Meddling

The beginning of strife is as when one letteth out water: therefore leave off contention, before it be meddled with.

Proverbs 17:14

Through desire a man, having separated himself, seeketh and intermeddleth with all wisdom. *Proverbs 18:1*

It is an honour for a man to cease from strife: but every fool will be meddling. *Proverbs 20:3*

He that goeth about as a talebearer revealeth secrets: therefore meddle not with him that flattereth with his lips.

Proverbs 20:19

My son, fear thou the LORD and the king: and meddle not with them that are given to change. *Proverbs 24:21*

He that passeth by, and meddleth with strife belonging not to him, is like one that taketh a dog by the ears.

Proverbs 26:17

Mercy

Let not mercy and truth forsake thee: bind them about thy neck; write them upon the table of thine heart: So shalt thou find favour and good understanding in the sight of God and man. *Proverbs 3:3–4*

The merciful man doeth good to his own soul: but he that is cruel troubleth his own flesh. *Proverbs 11:17*

A righteous man regardeth the life of his beast: but the tender mercies of the wicked are cruel. *Proverbs 12:10*

He that despiseth his neighbour sinneth: but he that hath mercy on the poor, happy is he. *Proverbs 14:21*

Do they not err that devise evil? but mercy and truth shall be to them that devise good. *Proverbs 14:22*

He that oppresseth the poor reproacheth his Maker: but he that honoureth him hath mercy on the poor.
Proverbs 14:31

By mercy and truth iniquity is purged: and by the fear of the LORD men depart from evil. *Proverbs 16:6*

He that hath pity upon the poor lendeth unto the LORD; and that which he hath given will he pay him again.

Proverbs 19:17

The desire of a man is his kindness: and a poor man is better than a liar.

Proverbs 19:22

Mercy and truth preserve the king: and his throne is upholden by mercy.

Proverbs 20:28

He that followeth after righteousness and mercy findeth life, righteousness, and honour.

Proverbs 21:21

He that by usury and unjust gain increaseth his substance, he shall gather it for him that will pity the poor.

Proverbs 28:8

He that covereth his sins shall not prosper: but whoso confesseth and forsaketh them shall have mercy.

Proverbs 28:13

Mischief

Enter not into the path of the wicked, and go not in the way of evil men. Avoid it, pass not by it, turn from it, and pass away. For they sleep not, except they have done mischief; and their sleep is taken away, unless they cause some to fall. For they eat the bread of wickedness, and drink the wine of violence.   *Proverbs 4:14–17*

He that winketh with the eye causeth sorrow: but a prating fool shall fall.   *Proverbs 10:10*

It is as sport to a fool to do mischief: but a man of understanding hath wisdom.   *Proverbs 10:23*

The righteousness of the upright shall deliver them: but transgressors shall be taken in their own naughtiness.
                                    Proverbs 11:6

He that diligently seeketh good procureth favour: but he that seeketh mischief, it shall come unto him.
                                    Proverbs 11:27

There shall no evil happen to the just: but the wicked shall be filled with mischief.   *Proverbs 12:21*

He that hath a froward heart findeth no good: and he that hath a perverse tongue falleth into mischief.

Proverbs 17:20

Be not thou envious against evil men, neither desire to be with them. For their heart studieth destruction, and their lips talk of mischief. *Proverbs 24:1–2*

He that deviseth to do evil shall be called a mischievous person. *Proverbs 24:8*

Lay not wait, O wicked man, against the dwelling of the righteous; spoil not his resting place: For a just man falleth seven times, and riseth up again: but the wicked shall fall into mischief. *Proverbs 24:15–16*

As a mad man who casteth firebrands, arrows, and death, So is the man that deceiveth his neighbour, and saith, Am not I in sport? *Proverbs 26:18–19*

Happy is the man that feareth alway: but he that hardeneth his heart shall fall into mischief. *Proverbs 28:14*

Mothers

My son, hear the instruction of thy father, and forsake not the law of thy mother: For they shall be an ornament of grace unto thy head, and chains about thy neck.   *Proverbs 1:8–9*

My son, keep thy father's commandment, and forsake not the law of thy mother: Bind them continually upon thine heart, and tie them about thy neck. When thou goest, it shall lead thee; when thou sleepest, it shall keep thee; and when thou awakest, it shall talk with thee.   *Proverbs 6:20–22*

A wise son maketh a glad father: but a foolish son is the heaviness of his mother.   *Proverbs 10:1*

A wise son maketh a glad father: but a foolish man despiseth his mother.   *Proverbs 15:20*

A foolish son is a grief to his father, and bitterness to her that bare him.   *Proverbs 17:25*

He that wasteth his father, and chaseth away his mother, is a son that causeth shame, and bringeth reproach.
Proverbs 19:26

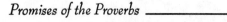

Whoso curseth his father or his mother, his lamp shall be put out in obscure darkness. *Proverbs 20:20*

Hearken unto thy father that begat thee, and despise not thy mother when she is old. *Proverbs 23:22*

The father of the righteous shall greatly rejoice: and he that begetteth a wise child shall have joy of him. Thy father and thy mother shall be glad, and she that bare thee shall rejoice. *Proverbs 23:24–25*

Whoso robbeth his father or his mother, and saith, It is no transgression; the same is the companion of a destroyer. *Proverbs 28:24*

The rod and reproof give wisdom: but a child left to himself bringeth his mother to shame. *Proverbs 29:15*

There is a generation that curseth their father, and doth not bless their mother. *Proverbs 30:11*

The eye that mocketh at his father, and despiseth to obey his mother, the ravens of the valley shall pick it out, and the young eagles shall eat it. *Proverbs 30:17*

Neighbors

Withhold not good from them to whom it is due, when it is in the power of thine hand to do it. Say not unto thy neighbour, Go, and come again, and to morrow I will give; when thou hast it by thee. Devise not evil against thy neighbour, seeing he dwelleth securely by thee.   *Proverbs 3:27–29*

An hypocrite with his mouth destroyeth his neighbour: but through knowledge shall the just be delivered.

Proverbs 11:9

He that is void of wisdom despiseth his neighbour: but a man of understanding holdeth his peace.   *Proverbs 11:12*

The righteous is more excellent than his neighbour: but the way of the wicked seduceth them.   *Proverbs 12:26*

The poor is hated even of his own neighbour: but the rich hath many friends.   *Proverbs 14:20*

He that despiseth his neighbour sinneth: but he that hath mercy on the poor, happy is he.   *Proverbs 14:21*

A violent man enticeth his neighbour, and leadeth him into the way that is not good. He shutteth his eyes to devise froward things: moving his lips he bringeth evil to pass.
Proverbs 16:29–30

He that is first in his own cause seemeth just; but his neighbour cometh and searcheth him. *Proverbs 18:17*

Wealth maketh many friends; but the poor is separated from his neighbour. *Proverbs 19:4*

The soul of the wicked desireth evil: his neighbour findeth no favour in his eyes. *Proverbs 21:10*

Be not a witness against thy neighbour without cause; and deceive not with thy lips. Say not, I will do so to him as he hath done to me: I will render to the man according to his work. *Proverbs 24:28–29*

Go not forth hastily to strive, lest thou know not what to do in the end thereof, when thy neighbour hath put thee to shame. Debate thy cause with thy neighbour himself; and discover not a secret to another: Lest he that heareth it put thee to shame, and thine infamy turn not away.
Proverbs 25:8–10

Withdraw thy foot from thy neighbour's house; lest he be weary of thee, and so hate thee.   *Proverbs 25:17*

A man that beareth false a witness against his neighbour is a maul, and a sword, and a sharp arrow.   *Proverbs 25:18*

As a mad man who casteth firebrands, arrows, and death, So is the man that deceiveth his neighbour, and saith, Am not I in sport?   *Proverbs 26:18–19*

Thine own friend, and thy father's friend, forsake not; neither go into thy brother's house in the day of thy calamity: for better is a neighbour that is near than a brother far off.
                                        Proverbs 27:10

A man that flattereth his neighbour spreadeth a net for his feet.   *Proverbs 29:5*

Oppression

Envy thou not the oppressor, and choose none of his ways.
Proverbs 3:31

He that oppresseth the poor reproacheth his Maker: but he that honoureth him hath mercy on the poor.
Proverbs 14:31

He that oppresseth the poor to increase his riches, and he that giveth to the rich, shall surely come to want.
Proverbs 22:16

Rob not the poor, because he is poor: neither oppress the afflicted in the gate: For the LORD will plead their cause, and spoil the soul of those that spoiled them.
Proverbs 22:22–23

A poor man that oppresseth the poor is like a sweeping rain which leaveth no food.
Proverbs 28:3

The prince that wanteth understanding is also a great oppressor: but he that hateth covetousness shall prolong his days.
Proverbs 28:16

Peace

My son, forget not my law; but let thine heart keep my commandments: For length of days, and long life, and peace, shall they add to thee.   *Proverbs 3:1–2*

Happy is the man that findeth wisdom, and the man that getteth understanding. For the merchandise of it is better than the merchandise of silver, and the gain thereof than fine gold. She is more precious than rubies: and all the things thou canst desire are not to be compared unto her. Length of days is in her right hand; and in her left hand riches and honour. Her ways are ways of pleasantness, and all her paths are peace.
                                        Proverbs 3:13–17

He that is void of wisdom despiseth his neighbour: but a man of understanding holdeth his peace.   *Proverbs 11:12*

Deceit is in the heart of them that imagine evil: but to the counsellors of peace is joy.   *Proverbs 12:20*

When a man's ways please the LORD, he maketh even his enemies to be at peace with him.   *Proverbs 16:7*

Perversity

When wisdom entereth into thine heart, and knowledge is pleasant unto thy soul; Discretion shall preserve thee, understanding shall keep thee: To deliver thee from the way of the evil man, from the man that speaketh froward things; Who leave the paths of uprightness, to walk in the ways of darkness; Who rejoice to do evil, and delight in the frowardness of the wicked; Whose ways are crooked, and they froward in their paths.   *Proverbs 2:10–15*

For the froward is abomination to the LORD: but his secret is with the righteous.   *Proverbs 3:32*

Keep thy heart with all diligence; for out of it are the issues of life. Put away from thee a froward mouth, and perverse lips put far from thee.   *Proverbs 4:23–24*

A naughty person, a wicked man, walketh with a froward mouth. He winketh with his eyes, he speaketh with his feet, he teacheth with his fingers; Frowardness is in his heart, he deviseth mischief continually; he soweth discord. Therefore shall his calamity come suddenly; suddenly shall he be broken without remedy.   *Proverbs 6:12–15*

Doth not wisdom cry? and understanding put forth her voice? . . .Unto you, O men, I call; and my voice is to the sons of man. . .Hear; for I will speak of excellent things; and the opening of my lips shall be right things. For my mouth shall speak truth; and wickedness is an abomination to my lips. All the words of my mouth are in righteousness; there is nothing froward or perverse in them.

Proverbs 8:1,4,6–8

The fear of the LORD is to hate evil: pride, and arrogancy, and the evil way, and the froward mouth, do I hate.

Proverbs 8:13

He that walketh uprightly walketh surely: but he that perverteth his ways shall be known.   *Proverbs 10:9*

The mouth of the just bringeth forth wisdom: but the froward tongue shall be cut out.   *Proverbs 10:31*

The lips of the righteous know what is acceptable: but the mouth of the wicked speaketh frowardness.

Proverbs 10:32

The integrity of the upright shall guide them: but the perverseness of transgressors shall destroy them.

Proverbs 11:3

They that are of a froward heart are abomination to the
LORD: but such as are upright in their way are his delight.
Proverbs 11:20

A man shall be commended according to his wisdom: but he
that is of a perverse heart shall be despised.
Proverbs 12:8

He that walketh in his uprightness feareth the LORD: but he
that is perverse in his ways despiseth him.   *Proverbs 14:2*

A wholesome tongue is a tree of life: but perverseness
therein is a breach in the spirit.   *Proverbs 15:4*

A froward man soweth strife: and a whisperer separateth
chief friends.   *Proverbs 16:28*

A violent man enticeth his neighbour, and leadeth him into
the way that is not good. He shutteth his eyes to devise
froward things: moving his lips he bringeth evil to pass.
Proverbs 16:29–30

He that hath a froward heart findeth no good: and he that
hath a perverse tongue falleth into mischief.
Proverbs 17:20

A wicked man taketh a gift out of the bosom to pervert the ways of judgment. *Proverbs 17:23*

Better is the poor that walketh in his integrity, than he that is perverse in his lips, and is a fool. *Proverbs 19:1*

The foolishness of man perverteth his way: and his heart fretteth against the LORD. *Proverbs 19:3*

The way of man is froward and strange: but as for the pure, his work is right. *Proverbs 21:8*

Thorns and snares are in the way of the froward: he that doth keep his soul shall be far from them.
Proverbs 22:5

Who hath woe? who hath sorrow? who hath contentions? who hath babbling? who hath wounds without cause? who hath redness of eyes? They that tarry long at the wine; they that go to seek mixed wine. . .Thine eyes shall behold strange women, and thine heart shall utter perverse things.
Proverbs 23:29–30,33

Better is the poor that walketh in his uprightness, than he that is perverse in his ways, though he be rich.
Proverbs 28:6

The Poor

He becometh poor that dealeth with a slack hand: but the hand of the diligent maketh rich. *Proverbs 10:4*

The rich man's wealth is his strong city: the destruction of the poor is their poverty. *Proverbs 10:15*

There is that maketh himself rich, yet hath nothing: there is that maketh himself poor, yet hath great riches.
Proverbs 13:7

The ransom of a man's life are his riches: but the poor heareth not rebuke. *Proverbs 13:8*

Much food is in the tillage of the poor: but there is that is destroyed for want of judgment. *Proverbs 13:23*

The poor is hated even of his own neighbour: but the rich hath many friends. *Proverbs 14:20*

He that despiseth his neighbour sinneth: but he that hath mercy on the poor, happy is he. *Proverbs 14:21*

He that oppresseth the poor reproacheth his Maker: but he that honoureth him hath mercy on the poor. *Proverbs 14:31*

Better is little with the fear of the LORD than great treasure and trouble therewith.   *Proverbs 15:16*

Better is a little with righteousness than great revenues without right.   *Proverbs 16:8*

Whoso mocketh the poor reproacheth his Maker: and he that is glad at calamities shall not be unpunished.

Proverbs 17:5

The poor useth intreaties; but the rich answereth roughly.

Proverbs 18:23

Better is the poor that walketh in his integrity, than he that is perverse in his lips, and is a fool.   *Proverbs 19:1*

Wealth maketh many friends; but the poor is separated from his neighbour.   *Proverbs 19:4*

All the brethren of the poor do hate him: how much more do his friends go far from him? he pursueth them with words, yet they are wanting to him.   *Proverbs 19:7*

He that hath pity upon the poor lendeth unto the LORD; and that which he hath given will he pay him again.

Proverbs 19:17

The desire of a man is his kindness: and a poor man is better than a liar. *Proverbs 19:22*

Whoso stoppeth his ears at the cry of the poor, he also shall cry himself, but shall not be heard. *Proverbs 21:13*

He that loveth pleasure shall be a poor man: he that loveth wine and oil shall not be rich. *Proverbs 21:17*

The rich and poor meet together: the LORD is the maker of them all. *Proverbs 22:2*

The rich ruleth over the poor, and the borrower is servant to the lender. *Proverbs 22:7*

He that hath a bountiful eye shall be blessed; for he giveth of his bread to the poor. *Proverbs 22:9*

He that oppresseth the poor to increase his riches, and he that giveth to the rich, shall surely come to want.
Proverbs 22:16

Rob not the poor, because he is poor: neither oppress the afflicted in the gate: For the LORD will plead their cause, and spoil the soul of those that spoiled them.
Proverbs 22:22–23

A poor man that oppresseth the poor is like a sweeping rain which leaveth no food. *Proverbs 28:3*

Better is the poor that walketh in his uprightness, than he that is perverse in his ways, though he be rich.

Proverbs 28:6

He that by usury and unjust gain increaseth his substance, he shall gather it for him that will pity the poor.

Proverbs 28:8

The rich man is wise in his own conceit; but the poor that hath understanding searcheth him out. *Proverbs 28:11*

As a roaring lion, and a ranging bear; so is a wicked ruler over the poor people. *Proverbs 28:15*

He that giveth unto the poor shall not lack: but he that hideth his eyes shall have many a curse. *Proverbs 28:27*

The righteous considereth the cause of the poor: but the wicked regardeth not to know it. *Proverbs 29:7*

The poor and the deceitful man meet together: the LORD lighteneth both their eyes. *Proverbs 29:13*

The king that faithfully judgeth the poor, his throne shall be established for ever.   *Proverbs 29:14*

There is a generation, whose teeth are as swords, and their jaw teeth as knives, to devour the poor from off the earth, and the needy from among men.   *Proverbs 30:14*

Open thy mouth for the dumb in the cause of all such as are appointed to destruction. Open thy mouth, judge righteously, and plead the cause of the poor and needy.

Proverbs 31:8–9

Poverty

For the lips of a strange woman drop as an honeycomb, and her mouth is smoother than oil. . .Remove thy way far from her, and come not nigh the door of her house: Lest thou give thine honour unto others, and thy years unto the cruel: Lest strangers be filled with thy wealth; and thy labours be in the house of a stranger.   *Proverbs 5:3,8–10*

How long wilt thou sleep, O sluggard? when wilt thou arise out of thy sleep? Yet a little sleep, a little slumber, a little folding of the hands to sleep: So shall thy poverty come as one that travelleth, and thy want as an armed man.
                                        Proverbs 6:9–11

For by means of a whorish woman a man is brought to a piece of bread: and the adulteress will hunt for the precious life.   *Proverbs 6:26*

The LORD will not suffer the soul of the righteous to famish: but he casteth away the substance of the wicked.
                                        Proverbs 10:3

There is that scattereth, and yet increaseth; and there is that withholdeth more than is meet, but it tendeth to poverty.
                                        Proverbs 11:24

He that is despised, and hath a servant, is better than he that honoureth himself, and lacketh bread.   *Proverbs 12:9*

Poverty and shame shall be to him that refuseth instruction: but he that regardeth reproof shall be honoured.

Proverbs 13:18

The righteous eateth to the satisfying of his soul: but the belly of the wicked shall want.   *Proverbs 13:25*

In all labour there is profit: but the talk of the lips tendeth only to penury.   *Proverbs 14:23*

Better is little with the fear of the LORD than great treasure and trouble therewith.   *Proverbs 15:16*

Better is a little with righteousness than great revenues without right.   *Proverbs 16:8*

The sluggard will not plow by reason of the cold; therefore shall he beg in harvest, and have nothing.   *Proverbs 20:4*

Love not sleep, lest thou come to poverty; open thine eyes, and thou shalt be satisfied with bread.   *Proverbs 20:13*

The thoughts of the diligent tend only to plenteousness; but of every one that is hasty only to want.   *Proverbs 21:5*

He that oppresseth the poor to increase his riches, and he that giveth to the rich, shall surely come to want.
Proverbs 22:16

Be not among winebibbers; among riotous eaters of flesh: For the drunkard and the glutton shall come to poverty: and drowsiness shall clothe a man with rags.
Proverbs 23:20–21

I went by the field of the slothful, and by the vineyard of the man void of understanding; And, lo, it was all grown over with thorns, and nettles had covered the face thereof, and the stone wall thereof was broken down. Then I saw, and considered it well: I looked upon it, and received instruction. Yet a little sleep, a little slumber, a little folding of the hands to sleep: So shall thy poverty come as one that travelleth; and thy want as an armed man.   *Proverbs 24:30–34*

He that tilleth his land shall have plenty of bread: but he that followeth after vain persons shall have poverty enough.
Proverbs 28:19

He that hasteth to be rich hath an evil eye, and considereth not that poverty shall come upon him.   *Proverbs 28:22*

Pride

These six things doth the LORD hate: yea, seven are an abomination unto him: A proud look, a lying tongue, and hands that shed innocent blood, An heart that deviseth wicked imaginations, feet that be swift in running to mischief. A false witness that speaketh lies, and he that soweth discord among brethren. *Proverbs 6:16–19*

The fear of the LORD is to hate evil: pride, and arrogancy, and the evil way, and the froward mouth, do I hate.
Proverbs 8:13

When pride cometh, then cometh shame: but with the lowly is wisdom. *Proverbs 11:2*

Only by pride cometh contention: but with the well advised is wisdom. *Proverbs 13:10*

In the mouth of the foolish is a rod of pride: but the lips of the wise shall preserve them. *Proverbs 14:3*

The LORD will destroy the house of the proud: but he will establish the border of the widow. *Proverbs 15:25*

Every one that is proud in heart is an abomination to the LORD: though hand join in hand, he shall not be unpunished. *Proverbs 16:5*

Pride goeth before destruction, and an haughty spirit before a fall. *Proverbs 16:18*

Better it is to be of an humble spirit with the lowly, than to divide the spoil with the proud. *Proverbs 16:19*

Before destruction the heart of man is haughty, and before honour is humility. *Proverbs 18:12*

An high look, and a proud heart, and the plowing of the wicked, is sin. *Proverbs 21:4*

Proud and haughty scorner is his name, who dealeth in proud wrath. *Proverbs 21:24*

Boast not thyself of to morrow; for thou knowest not what a day may bring forth. *Proverbs 27:1*

Let another man praise thee, and not thine own mouth; a stranger, and not thine own lips. *Proverbs 27:2*

As the fining pot for silver, and the furnace for gold; so is a man to his praise.   *Proverbs 27:21*

The rich man is wise in his own conceit; but the poor that hath understanding searcheth him out.   *Proverbs 28:11*

He that is of a proud heart stirreth up strife: but he that putteth his trust in the LORD shall be made fat.

Proverbs 28:25

A man's pride shall bring him low: but honour shall uphold the humble in spirit.   *Proverbs 29:23*

There is a generation, O how lofty are their eyes! and their eyelids are lifted up.   *Proverbs 30:13*

If thou hast done foolishly in lifting up thyself, or if thou hast thought evil, lay thine hand upon thy mouth.

Proverbs 30:32

Prosperity

For the turning away of the simple shall slay them, and the prosperity of fools shall destroy them. *Proverbs 1:32*

The blessing of the LORD, it maketh rich, and he addeth no sorrow with it. *Proverbs 10:22*

The liberal soul shall be made fat: and he that watereth shall be watered also himself. *Proverbs 11:25*

The house of the wicked shall be overthrown: but the tabernacle of the upright shall flourish. *Proverbs 14:11*

A gift is as a precious stone in the eyes of him that hath it: whithersoever it turneth, it prospereth. *Proverbs 17:8*

The thoughts of the diligent tend only to plenteousness; but of every one that is hasty only to want. *Proverbs 21:5*

He that by usury and unjust gain increaseth his substance, he shall gather it for him that will pity the poor.
Proverbs 28:8

He that covereth his sins shall not prosper: but whoso confesseth and forsaketh them shall have mercy.

Proverbs 28:13

He that tilleth his land shall have plenty of bread: but he that followeth after vain persons shall have poverty enough. *Proverbs 28:19*

A faithful man shall abound with blessings: but he that maketh haste to be rich shall not be innocent.

Proverbs 28:20

He that is of a proud heart stirreth up strife: but he that putteth his trust in the LORD shall be made fat.

Proverbs 28:25

Prudence

A fool's wrath is presently known: but a prudent man covereth shame.   *Proverbs 12:16*

A prudent man concealeth knowledge: but the heart of fools proclaimeth foolishness.   *Proverbs 12:23*

Every prudent man dealeth with knowledge: but a fool layeth open his folly.   *Proverbs 13:16*

The wisdom of the prudent is to understand his way: but the folly of fools is deceit.   *Proverbs 14:8*

The simple believeth every word: but the prudent man looketh well to his going.   *Proverbs 14:15*

The simple inherit folly: but the prudent are crowned with knowledge.   *Proverbs 14:18*

A fool despiseth his father's instruction: but he that regardeth reproof is prudent.   *Proverbs 15:5*

The wise in heart shall be called prudent: and the sweetness of the lips increaseth learning.   *Proverbs 16:21*

Punishment

A reproof entereth more into a wise man than an hundred stripes into a fool.
Proverbs 17:10

Also to punish the just is not good, nor to strike princes for equity.
Proverbs 17:26

A fool's lips enter into contention, and his mouth calleth for strokes.
Proverbs 18:6

A man of great wrath shall suffer punishment: for if thou deliver him, yet thou must do it again.
Proverbs 19:19

Judgments are prepared for scorners, and stripes for the back of fools.
Proverbs 19:29

A wise king scattereth the wicked, and bringeth the wheel over them.
Proverbs 20:26

The blueness of a wound cleanseth away evil: so do stripes the inward parts of the belly.
Proverbs 20:30

When the scorner is punished, the simple is made wise: and when the wise is instructed, he receiveth knowledge.
Proverbs 21:11

Purity

The thoughts of the wicked are an abomination to the LORD: but the words of the pure are pleasant words.

Proverbs 15:26

All the ways of a man are clean in his own eyes; but the LORD weigheth the spirits.

Proverbs 16:2

Who can say, I have made my heart clean, I am pure from my sin?

Proverbs 20:9

Even a child is known by his doings, whether his work be pure, and whether it be right.

Proverbs 20:11

The way of man is froward and strange: but as for the pure, his work is right.

Proverbs 21:8

He that loveth pureness of heart, for the grace of his lips the king shall be his friend.

Proverbs 22:11

Every word of God is pure: he is a shield unto them that put their trust in him. Add thou not unto his words, lest he reprove thee, and thou be found a liar.

Proverbs 30:5–6

Reproof & Correction

Wisdom crieth without; she uttereth her voice in the streets: She crieth in the chief place of concourse, in the openings of the gates: in the city she uttereth her words, saying, How long, ye simple ones, will ye love simplicity? and the scorners delight in their scorning, and fools hate knowledge? Turn you at my reproof: behold, I will pour out my spirit unto you, I will make known my words unto you. Because I have called, and ye refused; I have stretched out my hand, and no man regarded; But ye have set at nought all my counsel, and would none of my reproof: I also will laugh at your calamity; I will mock when your fear cometh; When your fear cometh as desolation, and your destruction cometh as a whirlwind; when distress and anguish cometh upon you. Then shall they call upon me, but I will not answer; they shall seek me early, but they shall not find me: For that they hated knowledge, and did not choose the fear of the LORD: They would none of my counsel: they despised all my reproof. Therefore shall they eat of the fruit of their own way, and be filled with their own devices. For the turning away of the simple shall slay them, and the prosperity of fools shall destroy them. But whoso hearkeneth unto me shall dwell safely, and shall be quiet from fear of evil.

Proverbs 1:20–33

My son, despise not the chastening of the LORD; neither be weary of his correction: For whom the LORD loveth he correcteth; even as a father the son in whom he delighteth.

Proverbs 3:11–12

How have I hated instruction, and my heart despised reproof;
And have not obeyed the voice of my teachers, nor inclined
mine ear to them that instructed me! I was almost in all evil
in the midst of the congregation and assembly.

Proverbs 5:12–14

For the commandment is a lamp; and the law is light; and
reproofs of instruction are the way of life: *Proverbs 6:23*

He that reproveth a scorner getteth to himself shame: and
he that rebuketh a wicked man getteth himself a blot.

Proverbs 9:7

Reprove not a scorner, lest he hate thee: rebuke a wise man,
and he will love thee.   *Proverbs 9:8*

Give instruction to a wise man, and he will be yet wiser:
teach a just man, and he will increase in learning.

Proverbs 9:9

The wise in heart will receive commandments: but a prating fool shall fall.   *Proverbs 10:8*

In the lips of him that hath understanding wisdom is found:
but a rod is for the back of him that is void of understanding.

Proverbs 10:13

He is in the way of life that keepeth instruction: but he that refuseth reproof erreth.   *Proverbs 10:17*

Whoso loveth instruction loveth knowledge: but he that hateth reproof is brutish.   *Proverbs 12:1*

The way of a fool is right in his own eyes: but he that hearkeneth unto counsel is wise.   *Proverbs 12:15*

A wise son heareth his father's instruction: but a scorner heareth not rebuke.   *Proverbs 13:1*

Whoso despiseth the word shall be destroyed: but he that feareth the commandment shall be rewarded.
                    Proverbs 13:13

Poverty and shame shall be to him that refuseth instruction: but he that regardeth reproof shall be honoured.
                    Proverbs 13:18

A fool despiseth his father's instruction: but he that regardeth reproof is prudent.   *Proverbs 15:5*

Correction is grievous unto him that forsaketh the way: and he that hateth reproof shall die.   *Proverbs 15:10*

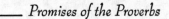

A scorner loveth not one that reproveth him: neither will he go unto the wise. _Proverbs 15:12_

The ear that heareth the reproof of life abideth among the wise. _Proverbs 15:31_

He that refuseth instruction despiseth his own soul: but he that heareth reproof getteth understanding.
Proverbs 15:32

A reproof entereth more into a wise man than an hundred stripes into a fool. _Proverbs 17:10_

Hear counsel, and receive instruction, that thou mayest be wise in thy latter end. _Proverbs 19:20_

Smite a scorner, and the simple will beware: and reprove one that hath understanding, and he will understand knowledge. _Proverbs 19:25_

Foolishness is bound in the heart of a child; but the rod of correction shall drive it far from him. _Proverbs 22:15_

Speak not in the ears of a fool: for he will despise the wisdom of thy words. _Proverbs 23:9_

Withhold not correction from the child: for if thou beatest him with the rod, he shall not die. *Proverbs 23:13*

He that saith unto the wicked, Thou art righteous; him shall the people curse, nations shall abhor him: But to them that rebuke him shall be delight, and a good blessing shall come upon them. *Proverbs 24:24–25*

A word fitly spoken is like apples of gold in pictures of silver. As an earring of gold, and an ornament of fine gold, so is a wise reprover upon an obedient ear. *Proverbs 25:11–12*

Answer a fool according to his folly, lest he be wise in his own conceit. *Proverbs 26:5*

Open rebuke is better than secret love. *Proverbs 27:5*

Faithful are the wounds of a friend; but the kisses of an enemy are deceitful. *Proverbs 27:6*

The full soul loatheth an honeycomb; but to the hungry soul every bitter thing is sweet. *Proverbs 27:7*

Though thou shouldest bray a fool in a mortar among wheat with a pestle, yet will not his foolishness depart from him. *Proverbs 27:22*

They that forsake the law praise the wicked: but such as keep the law contend with them.   *Proverbs 28:4*

He that rebuketh a man afterwards shall find more favour than he that flattereth with the tongue.   *Proverbs 28:23*

He, that being often reproved hardeneth his neck, shall suddenly be destroyed, and that without remedy.
                                             Proverbs 29:1

Reward

The wicked worketh a deceitful work: but to him that soweth righteousness shall be a sure reward.

Proverbs 11:18

Behold, the righteous shall be recompensed in the earth: much more the wicked and the sinner.   *Proverbs 11:31*

A man shall be satisfied with good by the fruit of his mouth: and the recompence of a man's hands shall be rendered unto him.   *Proverbs 12:14*

Whoso despiseth the word shall be destroyed: but he that feareth the commandment shall be rewarded.

Proverbs 13:13

Evil pursueth sinners: but to the righteous good shall be repayed.   *Proverbs 13:21*

Whoso rewardeth evil for good, evil shall not depart from his house.   *Proverbs 17:13*

A gift in secret pacifieth anger: and a reward in the bosom strong wrath.   *Proverbs 21:14*

My son, eat thou honey, because it is good; and the honey-comb, which is sweet to thy taste: So shall the knowledge of wisdom be unto thy soul: when thou hast found it, then there shall be a reward, and thy expectation shall not be cut off.   *Proverbs 24:13–14*

Fret not thyself because of evil men, neither be thou envious at the wicked; For there shall be no reward to the evil man; the candle of the wicked shall be put out.

Proverbs 24:19–20

If thine enemy be hungry, give him bread to eat; and if he be thirsty, give him water to drink: For thou shalt heap coals of fire upon his head, and the LORD shall reward thee.

Proverbs 25:21–22

The great God that formed all things both rewardeth the fool, and rewardeth transgressors.   *Proverbs 26:10*

The Rich

The rich man's wealth is his strong city: the destruction of the poor is their poverty.   *Proverbs 10:15*

He that trusteth in his riches shall fall: but the righteous shall flourish as a branch.   *Proverbs 11:28*

There is that maketh himself rich, yet hath nothing: there is that maketh himself poor, yet hath great riches.
Proverbs 13:7

The poor is hated even of his own neighbour: but the rich hath many friends.   *Proverbs 14:20*

Better is a dry morsel, and quietness therewith, than an house full of sacrifices with strife.   *Proverbs 17:1*

The rich man's wealth is his strong city, and as an high wall in his own conceit.   *Proverbs 18:11*

The poor useth intreaties; but the rich answereth roughly.
Proverbs 18:23

Wealth maketh many friends; but the poor is separated from his neighbour.
Proverbs 19:4

The rich and poor meet together: the LORD is the maker of them all.
Proverbs 22:2

The rich ruleth over the poor, and the borrower is servant to the lender.
Proverbs 22:7

He that oppresseth the poor to increase his riches, and he that giveth to the rich, shall surely come to want.
Proverbs 22:16

The rich man is wise in his own conceit; but the poor that hath understanding searcheth him out.
Proverbs 28:11

A faithful man shall abound with blessings: but he that maketh haste to be rich shall not be innocent.
Proverbs 28:20

Riches & Wealth

Honour the LORD with thy substance, and with the first-fruits of all thine increase: So shall thy barns be filled with plenty, and thy presses shall burst out with new wine.
Proverbs 3:9–10

Happy is the man that findeth wisdom, and the man that getteth understanding. For the merchandise of it is better than the merchandise of silver, and the gain thereof than fine gold. She is more precious than rubies: and all the things thou canst desire are not to be compared unto her. Length of days is in her right hand; and in her left hand riches and honour. *Proverbs 3:13–16*

Receive my instruction, and not silver; and knowledge rather than choice gold. For wisdom is better than rubies; and all the things that may be desired are not to be compared to it. . .Riches and honour are with me; yea, durable riches and righteousness My fruit is better than gold, yea, than fine gold; and my revenue than choice silver. I lead in the way of right-eousness, in the midst of the paths of judgment: That I may cause those that love me to inherit substance; and I will fill their treasures. *Proverbs 8:10–11, 18–21*

Treasures of wickedness profit nothing: but righteousness delivereth from death. *Proverbs 10:2*

The LORD will not suffer the soul of the righteous to famish: but he casteth away the substance of the wicked.

Proverbs 10:3

He becometh poor that dealeth with a slack hand: but the hand of the diligent maketh rich. *Proverbs 10:4*

The blessing of the LORD, it maketh rich, and he addeth no sorrow with it. *Proverbs 10:22*

Riches profit not in the day of wrath: but righteousness delivereth from death. *Proverbs 11:4*

A gracious woman retaineth honour: and strong men retain riches. *Proverbs 11:16*

He that trusteth in his riches shall fall: but the righteous shall flourish as a branch. *Proverbs 11:28*

The soul of the sluggard desireth, and hath nothing: but the soul of the diligent shall be made fat. *Proverbs 13:4*

There is that maketh himself rich, yet hath nothing: there is that maketh himself poor, yet hath great riches.

Proverbs 13:7

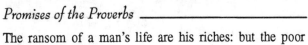

The ransom of a man's life are his riches: but the poor heareth not rebuke.   *Proverbs 13:8*

Wealth gotten by vanity shall be diminished: but he that gathereth by labour shall increase.   *Proverbs 13:11*

A good man leaveth an inheritance to his children's children: and the wealth of the sinner is laid up for the just.
                                        Proverbs 13:22

Where no oxen are, the crib is clean: but much increase is by the strength of the ox.   *Proverbs 14:4*

The crown of the wise is their riches: but the foolishness of fools is folly.   *Proverbs 14:24*

In the house of the righteous is much treasure: but in the revenues of the wicked is trouble.   *Proverbs 15:6*

He that is greedy of gain troubleth his own house; but he that hateth gifts shall live.   *Proverbs 15:27*

Better is a little with righteousness than great revenues without right.   *Proverbs 16:8*

How much better is it to get wisdom than gold! and to get understanding rather to be chosen than silver!

Proverbs 16:16

The rich man's wealth is his strong city, and as an high wall in his own conceit. *Proverbs 18:11*

A man's belly shall be satisified with the fruit of his mouth; and with the increase of his lips shall he be filled.

Proverbs 18:20

House and riches are the inheritance of fathers: and a prudent wife is from the LORD. *Proverbs 19:14*

There is gold, and a multitude of rubies: but the lips of knowledge are a precious jewel. *Proverbs 20:15*

The thoughts of the diligent tend only to plenteousness; but of every one that is hasty only to want. *Proverbs 21:5*

The getting of treasures by a lying tongue is a vanity tossed to and fro of them that seek death. *Proverbs 21:6*

He that loveth pleasure shall be a poor man: he that loveth wine and oil shall not be rich. *Proverbs 21:17*

A good name is rather to be chosen than great riches, and loving favour rather than silver and gold.   *Proverbs 22:1*

By humility and the fear of the LORD are riches, and honour, and life.   *Proverbs 22:4*

Labour not to be rich: cease from thine own wisdom. Wilt thou set thine eyes upon that which is not? for riches certainly make themselves wings; they fly away as an eagle toward heaven.   *Proverbs 23:4–5*

Through wisdom is an house builded; and by understanding it is established: And by knowledge shall the chambers be filled with all precious and pleasant riches.
    Proverbs 24:3–4

Be thou diligent to know the state of thy flocks, and look well to thy herds. For riches are not for ever: and doth the crown endure to every generation?   *Proverbs 27:23–24*

He that by usury and unjust gain increaseth his substance, he shall gather it for him that will pity the poor.
    Proverbs 28:8

He that hasteth to be rich hath an evil eye, and considereth not that poverty shall come upon him.   *Proverbs 28:22*

The Righteous
& The Just

For the froward is abomination to the LORD: but his secret is with the righteous. *Proverbs 3:32*

The curse of the LORD is in the house of the wicked: but he blesseth the habitation of the just. *Proverbs 3:33*

But the path of the just is as the shining light, that shineth more and more unto the perfect day. *Proverbs 4:18*

Give instruction to a wise man, and he will be yet wiser: teach a just man, and he will increase in learning.
Proverbs 9:9

The LORD will not suffer the soul of the righteous to famish: but he casteth away the substance of the wicked.
Proverbs 10:3

Blessings are upon the head of the just: but violence covereth the mouth of the wicked. *Proverbs 10:6*

The memory of the just is blessed: but the name of the wicked shall rot. *Proverbs 10:7*

The mouth of a righteous man is a well of life: but violence covereth the mouth of the wicked.   *Proverbs 10:11*

The labour of the righteous tendeth to life: the fruit of the wicked to sin.   *Proverbs 10:16*

The tongue of the just is as choice silver: the heart of the wicked is little worth.   *Proverbs 10:20*

The lips of the righteous feed many: but fools die for want of wisdom.   *Proverbs 10:21*

The fear of the wicked, it shall come upon him: but the desire of the righteous shall be granted.   *Proverbs 10:24*

As the whirlwind passeth, so is the wicked no more: but the righteous is an everlasting foundation.   *Proverbs 10:25*

The hope of the righteous shall be gladness: but the expectation of the wicked shall perish.   *Proverbs 10:28*

The righteous shall never be removed: but the wicked shall not inhabit the earth.   *Proverbs 10:30*

The mouth of the just bringeth forth wisdom: but the froward tongue shall be cut out.   *Proverbs 10:31*

The lips of the righteous know what is acceptable: but the mouth of the wicked speaketh frowardness.

Proverbs 10:32

The righteous is delivered out of trouble, and the wicked cometh in his stead. *Proverbs 11:8*

An hypocrite with his mouth destroyeth his neighbour: but through knowledge shall the just be delivered.

Proverbs 11:9

When it goeth well with the righteous, the city rejoiceth: and when the wicked perish, there is shouting.

Proverbs 11:10

Though hand join in hand, the wicked shall not be unpunished: but the seed of the righteous shall be delivered.

Proverbs 11:21

The desire of the righteous is only good: but the expectation of the wicked is wrath. *Proverbs 11:23*

He that trusteth in his riches shall fall: but the righteous shall flourish as a branch. *Proverbs 11:28*

The fruit of the righteous is a tree of life; and he that winneth souls is wise. *Proverbs 11:30*

Behold, the righteous shall be recompensed in the earth: much more the wicked and the sinner.   *Proverbs 11:31*

A man shall not be established by wickedness: but the root of the righteous shall not be moved.   *Proverbs 12:3*

The thoughts of the righteous are right: but the counsels of the wicked are deceit.   *Proverbs 12:5*

The wicked are overthrown, and are not: but the house of the righteous shall stand.   *Proverbs 12:7*

A righteous man regardeth the life of his beast: but the tender mercies of the wicked are cruel.   *Proverbs 12:10*

The wicked desireth the net of evil men: but the root of the righteous yieldeth fruit.   *Proverbs 12:12*

The wicked is snared by the transgression of his lips: but the just shall come out of trouble.   *Proverbs 12:13*

There shall no evil happen to the just: but the wicked shall be filled with mischief.   *Proverbs 12:21*

The righteous is more excellent than his neighbour: but the way of the wicked seduceth them.   *Proverbs 12:26*

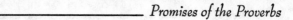

A righteous man hateth lying: but a wicked man is loath-some, and cometh to shame.   *Proverbs 13:5*

The light of the righteous rejoiceth: but the lamp of the wicked shall be put out.   *Proverbs 13:9*

Evil pursueth sinners: but to the righteous good shall be repayed.   *Proverbs 13:21*

A good man leaveth an inheritance to his children's chil-dren: and the wealth of the sinner is laid up for the just.
Proverbs 13:22

The righteous eateth to the satisfying of his soul: but the belly of the wicked shall want.   *Proverbs 13:25*

Fools make a mock at sin: but among the righteous there is favour.   *Proverbs 14:9*

The evil bow before the good; and the wicked at the gates of the righteous.   *Proverbs 14:19*

The wicked is driven away in his wickedness: but the right-eous hath hope in his death.   *Proverbs 14:32*

In the house of the righteous is much treasure: but in the revenues of the wicked is trouble.   *Proverbs 15:6*

The way of the slothful man is as an hedge of thorns: but the way of the righteous is made plain.   *Proverbs 15:19*

The heart of the righteous studieth to answer: but the mouth of the wicked poureth out evil things.   *Proverbs 15:28*

The LORD is far from the wicked: but he heareth the prayer of the righteous.   *Proverbs 15:29*

He that justifieth the wicked, and he that condemneth the just, even they both are abomination to the LORD.
          Proverbs 17:15

Also to punish the just is not good, nor to strike princes for equity.   *Proverbs 17:26*

It is not good to accept the person of the wicked, to over-throw the righteous in judgment.   *Proverbs 18:5*

The name of the LORD is a strong tower: the righteous run-neth into it, and is safe.   *Proverbs 18:10*

He that is first in his own cause seemeth just; but his neighbour cometh and searcheth him.　　　*Proverbs 18:17*

The just man walketh in his integrity: his children are blessed after him.　　　*Proverbs 20:7*

The righteous man wisely considereth the house of the wicked: but God overthroweth the wicked for their wickedness.　　　*Proverbs 21:12*

It is joy to the just to do judgment: but destruction shall be to the workers of iniquity.　　　*Proverbs 21:15*

The wicked shall be a ransom for the righteous, and the transgressor for the upright.　　　*Proverbs 21:18*

He coveteth greedily all the day long: but the righteous giveth and spareth not.　　　*Proverbs 21:26*

The father of the righteous shall greatly rejoice: and he that begetteth a wise child shall have joy of him.
　　　Proverbs 23:24

Lay not wait, O wicked man, against the dwelling of the righteous; spoil not his resting place: For a just man falleth seven times, and riseth up again: but the wicked shall fall into mischief.　　　*Proverbs 24:15–16*

A righteous man falling down before the wicked is as a troubled fountain, and a corrupt spring.   *Proverbs 25:26*

The wicked flee when no man pursueth: but the righteous are bold as a lion.   *Proverbs 28:1*

Whoso causeth the righteous to go astray in an evil way, he shall fall himself into his own pit: but the upright shall have good things in possession.   *Proverbs 28:10*

When righteous men do rejoice, there is great glory: but when the wicked rise, a man is hidden.   *Proverbs 28:12*

When the wicked rise, men hide themselves: but when they perish, the righteous increase.   *Proverbs 28:28*

When the righteous are in authority, the people rejoice: but when the wicked beareth rule, the people mourn.
                                                                                    Proverbs 29:2

In the transgression of an evil man there is a snare: but the righteous doth sing and rejoice.   *Proverbs 29:6*

The righteous considereth the cause of the poor: but the wicked regardeth not to know it.   *Proverbs 29:7*

Righteousness

All the words of my mouth are in righteousness; there is nothing froward or perverse in them. . .I lead in the way of righteousness, in the midst of the paths of judgment

Proverbs 8:8, 20

Treasures of wickedness profit nothing: but righteousness delivereth from death. *Proverbs 10:2*

Riches profit not in the day of wrath: but righteousness delivereth from death. *Proverbs 11:4*

The righteousness of the perfect shall direct his way: but the wicked shall fall by his own wickedness.

Proverbs 11:5

The righteousness of the upright shall deliver them: but transgressors shall be taken in their own naughtiness.

Proverbs 11:6

The wicked worketh a deceitful work: but to him that soweth righteousness shall be a sure reward.

Proverbs 11:18

As righteousness tendeth to life: so he that pursueth evil pursueth it to his own death. *Proverbs 11:19*

He that speaketh truth sheweth forth righteousness: but a false witness deceit. *Proverbs 12:17*

In the way of righteousness is life; and in the pathway thereof there is no death. *Proverbs 12:28*

Righteousness keepeth him that is upright in the way: but wickedness overthroweth the sinner. *Proverbs 13:6*

Righteousness exalteth a nation: but sin is a reproach to any people. *Proverbs 14:34*

The way of the wicked is an abomination unto the Lord: but he loveth him that followeth after righteousness.
Proverbs 15:9

Better is a little with righteousness than great revenues without right. *Proverbs 16:8*

It is an abomination to kings to commit wickedness: for the throne is established by righteousness. *Proverbs 16:12*

Righteous lips are the delight of kings; and they love him that speaketh right. *Proverbs 16:13*

The hoary head is a crown of glory, if it be found in the way of righteousness. *Proverbs 16:31*

To do justice and judgment is more acceptable to the LORD than sacrifice. *Proverbs 21:3*

The way of man is froward and strange: but as for the pure, his work is right. *Proverbs 21:8*

He that followeth after righteousness and mercy findeth life, righteousness, and honour. *Proverbs 21:21*

Take away the dross from the silver, and there shall come forth a vessel for the finer. Take away the wicked from before the king, and his throne shall be established in righteousness. *Proverbs 25:4–5*

Safety

For the turning away of the simple shall slay them, and the prosperity of fools shall destroy them. But whoso hearkeneth unto me shall dwell safely, and shall be quiet from fear of evil. *Proverbs 1:32–33*

My son, let not them depart from thine eyes: keep sound wisdom and discretion: So shall they be life unto thy soul, and grace to thy neck. Then shalt thou walk in thy way safely, and thy foot shall not stumble. *Proverbs 3:21–23*

Where no counsel is, the people fall: but in the multitude of counsellors there is safety. *Proverbs 11:14*

The name of the LORD is a strong tower: the righteous runneth into it, and is safe. *Proverbs 18:10*

The horse is prepared against the day of battle: but safety is of the LORD. *Proverbs 21:31*

For by wise counsel thou shalt make thy war: and in multitude of counsellors there is safety. *Proverbs 24:6*

Satisfaction

Let thy fountain be blessed: and rejoice with the wife of thy youth. Let her be as the loving hind and pleasant roe; let her breasts satisfy thee at all times; and be thou ravished always with her love. And why wilt thou, my son, be ravished with a strange woman, and embrace the bosom of a stranger?   *Proverbs 5:18–20*

He that tilleth his land shall be satisfied with bread: but he that followeth vain persons is void of understanding.
Proverbs 12:11

A man shall be satisfied with good by the fruit of his mouth: and the recompence of a man's hands shall be rendered unto him.   *Proverbs 12:14*

The righteous eateth to the satisfying of his soul: but the belly of the wicked shall want.   *Proverbs 13:25*

The backslider in heart shall be filled with his own ways: and a good man shall be satisfied from himself.
Proverbs 14:14

A man's belly shall be satisfied with the fruit of his mouth; and with the increase of his lips shall he be filled.
Proverbs 18:20

The fear of the LORD tendeth to life: and he that hath it shall abide satisfied; he shall not be visited with evil.

Proverbs 19:23

Love not sleep, lest thou come to poverty; open thine eyes, and thou shalt be satisfied with bread.   *Proverbs 20:13*

Hast thou found honey? eat so much as is sufficient for thee, lest thou be filled therewith, and vomit it.

Proverbs 25:16

Hell and destruction are never full; so the eyes of man are never satisfied.   *Proverbs 27:20*

He that tilleth his land shall have plenty of bread: but he that followeth after vain persons shall have poverty enough.   *Proverbs 28:19*

The horseleach hath two daughters, crying, Give, give. There are three things that are never satisfied, yea, four things say not, It is enough: The grave; and the barren womb; the earth that is not filled with water; and the fire that saith not, It is enough.   *Proverbs 30:15–16*

The Scorner

Surely he scorneth the scorners: but he giveth grace unto the lowly.   *Proverbs 3:34*

He that reproveth a scorner getteth to himself shame: and he that rebuketh a wicked man getteth himself a blot. Reprove not a scorner, lest he hate thee: rebuke a wise man, and he will love thee. Give instruction to a wise man, and he will be yet wiser: teach a just man, and he will increase in learning.   *Proverbs 9:7–9*

If thou be wise, thou shalt be wise for thyself: but if thou scornest, thou alone shalt bear it.   *Proverbs 9:12*

A wise son heareth his father's instruction: but a scorner heareth not rebuke.   *Proverbs 13:1*

A scorner seeketh wisdom, and findeth it not: but knowledge is easy unto him that understandeth.   *Proverbs 14:6*

Fools make a mock at sin: but among the righteous there is favour.   *Proverbs 14:9*

A scorner loveth not one that reproveth him: neither will he go unto the wise.   *Proverbs 15:12*

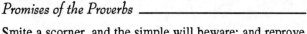

Smite a scorner, and the simple will beware: and reprove one that hath understanding, and he will understand knowledge. *Proverbs 19:25*

An ungodly witness scorneth judgment: and the mouth of the wicked devoureth iniquity. *Proverbs 19:28*

Judgments are prepared for scorners, and stripes for the back of fools. *Proverbs 19:29*

Wine is a mocker, strong drink is raging: and whosoever is deceived thereby is not wise. *Proverbs 20:1*

When the scorner is punished, the simple is made wise: and when the wise is instructed, he receiveth knowledge.

Proverbs 21:11

Proud and haughty scorner is his name, who dealeth in proud wrath. *Proverbs 21:24*

Cast out the scorner, and contention shall go out; yea, strife and reproach shall cease. *Proverbs 22:10*

Self-Control

Keep thy heart with all diligence; for out of it are the issues of life. *Proverbs 4:23*

In the multitude of words there wanteth not sin: but he that refraineth his lips is wise. *Proverbs 10:19*

A fool's wrath is presently known: but a prudent man covereth shame. *Proverbs 12:16*

The heart of the righteous studieth to answer: but the mouth of the wicked poureth out evil things. *Proverbs 15:28*

The preparations of the heart in man, and the answer of the tongue, is from the LORD. *Proverbs 16:1*

He that is slow to anger is better than the mighty; and he that ruleth his spirit than he that taketh a city.
Proverbs 16:32

He that hath knowledge spareth his words: and a man of understanding is of an excellent spirit. *Proverbs 17:27*

Even a fool, when he holdeth his peace, is counted wise: and he that shutteth his lips is esteemed a man of under- standing.   *Proverbs 17:28*

He that hath no rule over his own spirit is like a city that is broken down, and without walls.   *Proverbs 25:28*

A fool uttereth all his mind: but a wise man keepeth it in till afterwards.   *Proverbs 29:11*

Seest thou a man that is hasty in his words? there is more hope of a fool than of him.   *Proverbs 29:20*

If thou hast done foolishly in lifting up thyself, or if thou hast thought evil, lay thine hand upon thy mouth.
Proverbs 30:32

Self-Deception

Trust in the LORD with all thine heart; and lean not unto thine own understanding. In all thy ways acknowledge him, and he shall direct thy paths. Be not wise in thine own eyes: fear the LORD, and depart from evil.   *Proverbs 3:5–7*

The way of a fool is right in his own eyes: but he that hearkeneth unto counsel is wise.   *Proverbs 12:15*

There is a way which seemeth right unto a man, but the end thereof are the ways of death.   *Proverbs 14:12*

A wise man feareth, and departeth from evil: but the fool rageth, and is confident.   *Proverbs 14:16*

All the ways of a man are clean in his own eyes; but the LORD weigheth the spirits.   *Proverbs 16:2*

The rich man's wealth is his strong city, and as an high wall in his own conceit.   *Proverbs 18:11*

Most men will proclaim every one his own goodness: but a faithful man who can find?   *Proverbs 20:6*

Who can say, I have made my heart clean, I am pure from my sin?   *Proverbs 20:9*

Man's goings are of the LORD; how can a man then understand his own way?   *Proverbs 20 24*

Every way of a man is right in his own eyes: but the LORD pondereth the hearts.   *Proverbs 21:2*

Answer a fool according to his folly, lest he be wise in his own conceit.   *Proverbs 26:5*

Seest thou a man wise in his own conceit? There is more hope of a fool than of him.   *Proverbs 26:12*

The sluggard is wiser in his own conceit than seven men that can render a reason.   *Proverbs 26:16*

The rich man is wise in his own conceit; but the poor that hath understanding searcheth him out.   *Proverbs 28:11*

He that trusteth in his own heart is a fool: but whoso walketh wisely, he shall be delivered.   *Proverbs 28:26*

There is a generation that are pure in their own eyes, and yet is not washed from their filthiness.   *Proverbs 30:12*

Shame

The wise shall inherit glory: but shame shall be the promotion of fools. *Proverbs 3:35*

He that reproveth a scorner getteth to himself shame: and he that rebuketh a wicked man getteth himself a blot. *Proverbs 9:7*

He that gathereth in summer is a wise son: but he that sleepeth in harvest is a son that causeth shame. *Proverbs 10:5*

When pride cometh, then cometh shame: but with the lowly is wisdom. *Proverbs 11:2*

A virtuous woman is a crown to her husband: but she that maketh ashamed is as rottenness in his bones. *Proverbs 12:4*

A fool's wrath is presently known: but a prudent man covereth shame. *Proverbs 12:16*

A righteous man hateth lying: but a wicked man is loathsome, and cometh to shame. *Proverbs 13:5*

Poverty and shame shall be to him that refuseth instruction: but he that regardeth reproof shall be honoured.

Proverbs 13:18

The king's favour is toward a wise servant: but his wrath is against him that causeth shame. *Proverbs 14:35*

A wise servant shall have rule over a son that causeth shame, and shall have part of the inheritance among the brethren. *Proverbs 17:2*

When the wicked cometh, then cometh also contempt, and with ignominy reproach. *Proverbs 18:3*

He that answereth a matter before he heareth it, it is folly and shame unto him. *Proverbs 18:13*

He that wasteth his father, and chaseth away his mother, is a son that causeth shame, and bringeth reproach.

Proverbs 19:26

Go not forth hastily to strive, lest thou know not what to do in the end thereof, when thy neighbour hath put thee to shame. Debate thy cause with thy neighbour himself; and discover not a secret to another: Lest he that heareth it put thee to shame, and thine infamy turn not away.

Proverbs 25:8–10

My son, be wise, and make my heart glad, that I may answer him that reproacheth me.   *Proverbs 27:11*

Whoso keepeth the law is a wise son: but he that is a companion of riotous men shameth his father.   *Proverbs 28:7*

The rod and reproof give wisdom: but a child left to himself bringeth his mother to shame.   *Proverbs 29:15*

A man's pride shall bring him low: but honour shall uphold the humble in spirit.   *Proverbs 29:23*

Sickness

The merciful man doeth good to his own soul: but he that is cruel troubleth his own flesh. *Proverbs 11:17*

A virtuous woman is a crown to her husband: but she that maketh ashamed is as rottenness in his bones.
Proverbs 12:4

Hope deferred maketh the heart sick: but when the desire cometh, it is a tree of life. *Proverbs 13:12*

A sound heart is the life of the flesh: but envy the rottenness of the bones. *Proverbs 14:30*

A merry heart doeth good like a medicine: but a broken spirit drieth the bones. *Proverbs 17:22*

The Simple

For the turning away of the simple shall slay them, and the prosperity of fools shall destroy them.   *Proverbs 1:32*

O ye simple, understand wisdom: and, ye fools, be ye of an understanding heart.   *Proverbs 8:5*

Wisdom hath builded her house, she hath hewn out her seven pillars: She hath killed her beasts; she hath mingled her wine; she hath also furnished her table. She hath sent forth her maidens: she crieth upon the highest places of the city, Whoso is simple, let him turn in hither: as for him that wanteth understanding, she saith to him, Come, eat of my bread, and drink of the wine which I have mingled. Forsake the foolish, and live; and go in the way of understanding.   *Proverbs 9:1–6*

A foolish woman is clamorous: she is simple, and knoweth nothing. For she sitteth at the door of her house, on a seat in the high places of the city, To call passengers who go right on their ways: Whoso is simple, let him turn in hither: and as for him that wanteth understanding, she saith to him, Stolen waters are sweet, and bread eaten in secret is pleasant. But he knoweth not that the dead are there; and that her guests are in the depths of hell.   *Proverbs 9:13–18*

The simple believeth every word: but the prudent man looketh well to his going.   *Proverbs 14:15*

The simple inherit folly: but the prudent are crowned with knowledge.   *Proverbs 14:18*

Smite a scorner, and the simple will beware: and reprove one that hath understanding, and he will understand knowledge.   *Proverbs 19:25*

When the scorner is punished, the simple is made wise: and when the wise is instructed, he receiveth knowledge.
                    Proverbs 21:11

A prudent man foreseeth the evil, and hideth himself: but the simple pass on, and are punished.
                    Proverbs 22:3

Sin

My son, if sinners entice thee, consent thou not. If they say, Come with us, let us lay wait for blood, let us lurk privily for the innocent without cause: Let us swallow them up alive as the grave; and whole, as those that go down into the pit: We shall find all precious substance, we shall fill our houses with spoil: Cast in thy lot among us; let us all have one purse: My son, walk not thou in the way with them; refrain thy foot from their path: For their feet run to evil, and make haste to shed blood. Surely in vain the net is spread in the sight of any bird. And they lay wait for their own blood; they lurk privily for their own lives. So are the ways of every one that is greedy of gain; which taketh away the life of the owners thereof.

Proverbs 1:10–19

His own iniquities shall take the wicked himself, and he shall be holden with the cords of his sins. He shall die without instruction; and in the greatness of his folly he shall go astray. *Proverbs 5:22–23*

Now therefore hearken unto me, O ye children: for blessed are they that keep my ways. Hear instruction, and be wise, and refuse it not. Blessed is the man that heareth me, watching daily at my gates, waiting at the posts of my doors. For whoso findeth me findeth life, and shall obtain favour of the LORD. But he that sinneth against me wrongeth his own soul: all they that hate me love death. *Proverbs 8:32–36*

Hatred stirreth up strifes: but love covereth all sins.
Proverbs 10:12

The labour of the righteous tendeth to life: the fruit of the wicked to sin. *Proverbs 10:16*

In the multitude of words there wanteth not sin: but he that refraineth his lips is wise. *Proverbs 10:19*

Fools make a mock at sin: but among the righteous there is favour. *Proverbs 14:9*

He that despiseth his neighbour sinneth: but he that hath mercy on the poor, happy is he. *Proverbs 14:21*

Righteousness exalteth a nation: but sin is a reproach to any people. *Proverbs 14:34*

Also, that the soul be without knowledge, it is not good; and he that hasteth with his feet sinneth. *Proverbs 19:2*

The fear of a king is as the roaring of a lion: whoso provoketh him to anger sinneth against his own soul.
Proverbs 20:2

Who can say, I have made my heart clean, I am pure from my sin? *Proverbs 20:9*

Slothfulness

Go to the ant, thou sluggard; consider her ways, and be wise: Which having no guide, overseer, or ruler, Provideth her meat in the summer, and gathereth her food in the harvest. How long wilt thou sleep, O sluggard? when wilt thou arise out of thy sleep?   *Proverbs 6:6–9*

He becometh poor that dealeth with a slack hand: but the hand of the diligent maketh rich.   *Proverbs 10:4*

He that gathereth in summer is a wise son: but he that sleepeth in harvest is a son that causeth shame.
                                                        Proverbs 10:5

As vinegar to the teeth, and as smoke to the eyes, so is the sluggard to them that send him.   *Proverbs 10:26*

The hand of the diligent shall bear rule: but the slothful shall be under tribute.   *Proverbs 12:24*

The slothful man roasteth not that which he took in hunting: but the substance of a diligent man is precious.
                                                        Proverbs 12:27

The soul of the sluggard desireth, and hath nothing: but the soul of the diligent shall be made fat.   *Proverbs 13:4*

The way of the slothful man is as an hedge of thorns: but the way of the righteous is made plain.   *Proverbs 15:19*

He also that is slothful in his work is brother to him that is a great waster.   *Proverbs 18:9*

Slothfulness casteth into a deep sleep; and an idle soul shall suffer hunger.   *Proverbs 19:15*

A slothful man hideth his hand in his bosom, and will not so much as bring it to his mouth again.   *Proverbs 19:24*

The sluggard will not plow by reason of the cold; therefore shall he beg in harvest, and have nothing.   *Proverbs 20:4*

The desire of the slothful killeth him; for his hands refuse to labour. He coveteth greedily all the day long: but the righteous giveth and spareth not.   *Proverbs 21:25–26*

The slothful man saith, There is a lion without, I shall be slain in the streets.   *Proverbs 22:13*

I went by the field of the slothful, and by the vineyard of the man void of understanding; And, lo, it was all grown over with thorns, and nettles had covered the face thereof, and the stone wall thereof was broken down. Then I saw, and considered it well: I looked upon it, and received instruction. Yet a little sleep, a little slumber, a little folding of the hands to sleep: So shall thy poverty come as one that travelleth; and thy want as an armed man.

Proverbs 24:30–34

The slothful man saith, There is a lion in the way; a lion is in the streets. *Proverbs 26:13*

As the door turneth upon his hinges, so doth the slothful upon his bed. *Proverbs 26:14*

The slothful hideth his hand in his bosom; it grieveth him to bring it again to his mouth. *Proverbs 26:15*

The sluggard is wiser in his own conceit than seven men that can render a reason. *Proverbs 26:16*

Speech

Keep thy heart with all diligence; for out of it are the issues of life. Put away from thee a froward mouth, and perverse lips put far from thee.   *Proverbs 4:23–24*

Thou art snared with the words of thy mouth, thou art taken with the words of thy mouth.   *Proverbs 6:2*

A naughty person, a wicked man, walketh with a froward mouth.   *Proverbs 6:12*

Blessings are upon the head of the just: but violence covereth the mouth of the wicked.   *Proverbs 10:6*

The wise in heart will receive commandments: but a prating fool shall fall.   *Proverbs 10:8*

The mouth of a righteous man is a well of life: but violence covereth the mouth of the wicked.   *Proverbs 10:11*

In the lips of him that hath understanding wisdom is found: but a rod is for the back of him that is void of understanding.   *Proverbs 10:13*

Wise men lay up knowledge: but the mouth of the foolish is near destruction. *Proverbs 10:14*

He that hideth hatred with lying lips, and he that uttereth a slander, is a fool. *Proverbs 10:18*

In the multitude of words there wanteth not sin: but he that refraineth his lips is wise. *Proverbs 10:19*

The tongue of the just is as choice silver: the heart of the wicked is little worth. *Proverbs 10:20*

The lips of the righteous feed many: but fools die for want of wisdom. *Proverbs 10:21*

The mouth of the just bringeth forth wisdom: but the froward tongue shall be cut out. *Proverbs 10:31*

The lips of the righteous know what is acceptable: but the mouth of the wicked speaketh frowardness.

Proverbs 10:32

An hypocrite with his mouth destroyeth his neighbour: but through knowledge shall the just be delivered.

Proverbs 11:9

By the blessing of the upright the city is exalted: but it is overthrown by the mouth of the wicked.   *Proverbs 11:11*

He that is void of wisdom despiseth his neighbour: but a man of understanding holdeth his peace.   *Proverbs 11:12*

A talebearer revealeth secrets: but he that is of a faithful spirit concealeth the matter.   *Proverbs 11:13*

The words of the wicked are to lie in wait for blood: but the mouth of the upright shall deliver them.   *Proverbs 12:6*

The wicked is snared by the transgression of his lips: but the just shall come out of trouble.   *Proverbs 12:13*

A man shall be satisfied with good by the fruit of his mouth: and the recompence of a man's hands shall be rendered unto him.   *Proverbs 12:14*

He that speaketh truth sheweth forth righteousness: but a false witness deceit.   *Proverbs 12:17*

There is that speaketh like the piercings of a sword: but the tongue of the wise is health.   *Proverbs 12:18*

The lip of truth shall be established for ever: but a lying tongue is but for a moment.   *Proverbs 12:19*

Lying lips are abomination to the LORD: but they that deal truly are his delight.   *Proverbs 12:22*

A prudent man concealeth knowledge: but the heart of fools proclaimeth foolishness.   *Proverbs 12:23*

Heaviness in the heart of man maketh it stoop: but a good word maketh it glad.   *Proverbs 12:25*

A man shall eat good by the fruit of his mouth: but the soul of the transgressors shall eat violence.   *Proverbs 13:2*

He that keepeth his mouth keepeth his life: but he that openeth wide his lips shall have destruction.

Proverbs 13:3

In the mouth of the foolish is a rod of pride: but the lips of the wise shall preserve them.   *Proverbs 14:3*

Go from the presence of a foolish man, when thou perceivest not in him the lips of knowledge.   *Proverbs 14:7*

In all labour there is profit: but the talk of the lips tendeth only to penury. *Proverbs 14:23*

A soft answer turneth away wrath: but grievous words stir up anger. *Proverbs 15:1*

The tongue of the wise useth knowledge aright: but the mouth of fools poureth out foolishness. *Proverbs 15:2*

A wholesome tongue is a tree of life: but perverseness therein is a breach in the spirit. *Proverbs 15:4*

The lips of the wise disperse knowledge: but the heart of the foolish doeth not so. *Proverbs 15:7*

The heart of him that hath understanding seeketh knowledge: but the mouth of fools feedeth on foolishness.
Proverbs 15:14

A man hath joy by the answer of his moutn: and a word spoken in due season, how good is it! *Proverbs 15:23*

The thoughts of the wicked are an abomination to the LORD: but the words of the pure are pleasant words.
Proverbs 15:26

The heart of the righteous studieth to answer: but the mouth of the wicked poureth out evil things. *Proverbs 15:28*

The preparations of the heart in man, and the answer of the tongue, is from the LORD. *Proverbs 16:1*

A divine sentence is in the lips of the king: his mouth transgresseth not in judgment. *Proverbs 16:10*

Righteous lips are the delight of kings; and they love him that speaketh right. *Proverbs 16:13*

The wise in heart shall be called prudent: and the sweetness of the lips increaseth learning. *Proverbs 16:21*

The heart of the wise teacheth his mouth, and addeth learning to his lips. *Proverbs 16:23*

Pleasant words are as an honeycomb, sweet to the soul, and health to the bones. *Proverbs 16:24*

An ungodly man diggeth up evil: and in his lips there is as a burning fire. *Proverbs 16:27*

A wicked doer giveth heed to false lips; and a liar giveth ear to a naughty tongue. *Proverbs 17:4*

Excellent speech becometh not a fool: much less do lying lips a prince. *Proverbs 17:7*

He that hath a froward heart findeth no good: and he that hath a perverse tongue falleth into mischief.

Proverbs 17:20

He that hath knowledge spareth his words: and a man of understanding is of an excellent spirit. *Proverbs 17:27*

Even a fool, when he holdeth his peace, is counted wise: and he that shutteth his lips is esteemed a man of understanding. *Proverbs 17:28*

The words of a man's mouth are as deep waters, and the wellspring of wisdom as a flowing brook. *Proverbs 18:4*

A fool's lips enter into contention, and his mouth calleth for strokes. *Proverbs 18:6*

A fool's mouth is his destruction, and his lips are the snare of his soul. *Proverbs 18:7*

He that answereth a matter before he heareth it, it is folly and shame unto him. *Proverbs 18:13*

A man's belly shall be satisfied with the fruit of his mouth; and with the increase of his lips shall he be filled.

Proverbs 18:20

Death and life are in the power of the tongue: and they that love it shall eat the fruit thereof.   *Proverbs 18:21*

Better is the poor that walketh in his integrity, than he that is perverse in his lips, and is a fool.   *Proverbs 19:1*

A false witness shall not be unpunished, and he that speaketh lies shall not escape.   *Proverbs 19:5*

A false witness shall not be unpunished, and he that speaketh lies shall perish.   *Proverbs 19:9*

An ungodly witness scorneth judgment: and the mouth of the wicked devoureth iniquity.   *Proverbs 19:28*

There is gold, and a multitude of rubies: but the lips of knowledge are a precious jewel.   *Proverbs 20:15*

He that goeth about as a talebearer revealeth secrets: therefore meddle not with him that flattereth with his lips.

Proverbs 20:19

The getting of treasures by a lying tongue is a vanity tossed to and fro of them that seek death.   *Proverbs 21:6*

Whoso keepeth his mouth and his tongue keepeth his soul from troubles.   *Proverbs 21:23*

A false witness shall perish: but the man that heareth speaketh constantly.   *Proverbs 21:28*

He that loveth pureness of heart, for the grace of his lips the king shall be his friend.   *Proverbs 22:11*

The mouth of strange women is a deep pit: he that is abhorred of the LORD shall fall therein.   *Proverbs 22:14*

Bow down thine ear, and hear the words of the wise, and apply thine heart unto my knowledge. For it is a pleasant thing if thou keep them within thee; they shall withal be fitted in thy lips.   *Proverbs 22:17–18*

Speak not in the ears of a fool: for he will despise the wisdom of thy words.   *Proverbs 23:9*

My son, if thine heart be wise, my heart shall rejoice, even mine. Yea, my reins shall rejoice, when thy lips speak right things.   *Proverbs 23:15–16*

Be not thou envious against evil men, neither desire to be with them. For their heart studieth destruction, and their lips talk of mischief.   *Proverbs 24:1–2*

Wisdom is too high for a fool: he openeth not his mouth in the gate.   *Proverbs 24:7*

Every man shall kiss his lips that giveth a right answer.
                    Proverbs 24:26

Be not a witness against thy neighbour without cause; and deceive not with thy lips.   *Proverbs 24:28*

A word fitly spoken is like apples of gold in pictures of silver.   *Proverbs 25:11*

By long forbearing is a prince persuaded, and a soft tongue breaketh the bone.   *Proverbs 25:15*

The north wind driveth away rain: so doth an angry countenance a backbiting tongue.   *Proverbs 25:23*

The legs of the lame are not equal: so is a parable in the mouth of fools.   *Proverbs 26:7*

As a thorn goeth up into the hand of a drunkard, so is a parable in the mouth of fools.   *Proverbs 26:9*

Burning lips and a wicked heart are like a potsherd covered with silver dross. *Proverbs 26:23*

He that hateth dissembleth with his lips, and layeth up deceit within him; When he speaketh fair, believe him not: for there are seven abominations in his heart.
Proverbs 26:24–25

A lying tongue hateth those that are afflicted by it; and a flattering mouth worketh ruin. *Proverbs 26:28*

Let another man praise thee, and not thine own mouth; a stranger, and not thine own lips. *Proverbs 27:2*

He that rebuketh a man afterwards shall find more favour than he that flattereth with the tongue. *Proverbs 28:23*

Spirit of Man

A wholesome tongue is a tree of life: but perverseness therein is a breach in the spirit. *Proverbs 15:4*

A merry heart maketh a cheerful countenance: but by sorrow of the heart the spirit is broken. *Proverbs 15:13*

He that is slow to anger is better than the mighty; and he that ruleth his spirit than he that taketh a city.
Proverbs 16:32

A merry heart doeth good like a medicine: but a broken spirit drieth the bones. *Proverbs 17:22*

He that hath knowledge spareth his words: and a man of understanding is of an excellent spirit. *Proverbs 17:27*

The spirit of a man will sustain his infirmity; but a wounded spirit who can bear? *Proverbs 18:14*

The spirit of man is the candle of the LORD, searching all the inward parts of the belly. *Proverbs 20:27*

Strength

The fear of the LORD is to hate evil: pride, and arrogancy, and the evil way, and the froward mouth, do I hate. Counsel is mine, and sound wisdom: I am understanding; I have strength. *Proverbs 8:13–14*

The way of the LORD is strength to the upright: but destruction shall be to the workers of iniquity. *Proverbs 10:29*

A gracious woman retaineth honour: and strong men retain riches. *Proverbs 11:16*

Where no oxen are, the crib is clean: but much increase is by the strength of the ox. *Proverbs 14:4*

He that is slow to anger is better than the mighty; and he that ruleth his spirit than he that taketh a city.
Proverbs 16:32

The name of the LORD is a strong tower: the righteous runneth into it, and is safe. *Proverbs 18:10*

The rich man's wealth is his strong city, and as an high wall in his own conceit. *Proverbs 18:11*

The lot causeth contentions to cease, and parteth between the mighty.   *Proverbs 18:18*

The glory of young men is their strength: and the beauty of old men is the gray head.   *Proverbs 20:29*

A wise man scaleth the city of the mighty, and casteth down the strength of the confidence thereof.   *Proverbs 21:22*

A wise man is strong; yea, a man of knowledge increaseth strength.   *Proverbs 24:5*

If thou faint in the day of adversity, thy strength is small.
Proverbs 24:10

There be four things which are little upon the earth, but they are exceeding wise: The ants are a people not strong, yet they prepare their meat in the summer; The conies are but a feeble folk, yet make they their houses in the rocks; The locusts have no king, yet go they forth all of them by bands; The spider taketh hold with her hands, and is in kings' palaces.   *Proverbs 30:24–28*

Strife & Contention

Strive not with a man without cause, if he have done thee no harm. *Proverbs 3:30*

A naughty person, a wicked man, walketh with a froward mouth. He winketh with his eyes, he speaketh with his feet, he teacheth with his fingers; Frowardness is in his heart, he deviseth mischief continually; he soweth discord. Therefore shall his calamity come suddenly; suddenly shall he be broken without remedy. *Proverbs 6:12–15*

Hatred stirreth up strifes: but love covereth all sins. *Proverbs 10:12*

A wrathful man stirreth up strife: but he that is slow to anger appeaseth strife. *Proverbs 15:18*

A froward man soweth strife: and a whisperer separateth chief friends. *Proverbs 16:28*

Better is a dry morsel, and quietness therewith, than an house full of sacrifices with strife. *Proverbs 17:1*

The beginning of strife is as when one letteth out water: therefore leave off contention, before it be meddled with. *Proverbs 17:14*

He loveth transgression that loveth strife: and he that exalteth his gate seeketh destruction. *Proverbs 17:19*

A fool's lips enter into contention, and his mouth calleth for strokes. *Proverbs 18:6*

The lot causeth contentions to cease, and parteth between the mighty. *Proverbs 18:18*

A brother offended is harder to be won than a strong city: and their contentions are like the bars of a castle. *Proverbs 18:19*

A foolish son is the calamity of his father: and the contentions of a wife are a continual dropping. *Proverbs 19:13*

It is an honour for a man to cease from strife: but every fool will be meddling. *Proverbs 20:3*

It is better to dwell in a corner of the housetop, than with a brawling woman in a wide house. *Proverbs 21:9*

It is better to dwell in the wilderness, than with a contentious and an angry woman. *Proverbs 21:19*

Cast out the scorner, and contention shall go out; yea, strife and reproach shall cease. *Proverbs 22:10*

Who hath woe? who hath sorrow? who hath contentions? who hath babbling? who hath wounds without cause? who hath redness of eyes? They that tarry long at the wine; they that go to seek mixed wine. *Proverbs 23:29–30*

Go not forth hastily to strive, lest thou know not what to do in the end thereof, when thy neighbour hath put thee to shame. Debate thy cause with thy neighbour himself; and discover not a secret to another: Lest he that heareth it put thee to shame, and thine infamy turn not away.

Proverbs 25:8–10

It is better to dwell in the corner of the housetop, than with a brawling woman and in a wide house. *Proverbs 25:24*

He that passeth by, and meddleth with strife belonging not to him, is like one that taketh a dog by the ears.

Proverbs 26:17

Where no wood is, there the fire goeth out: so where there is no talebearer, the strife ceaseth. *Proverbs 26:20*

As coals are to burning coals, and wood to fire; so is a contentious man to kindle strife. *Proverbs 26:21*

A continual dropping in a very rainy day and a contentious woman are alike. Whosoever hideth her hideth the wind, and the ointment of his right hand, which bewrayeth itself.

Proverbs 27:15–16

He that is of a proud heart stirreth up strife: but he that putteth his trust in the LORD shall be made fat.

Proverbs 28:25

If a wise man contendeth with a foolish man, whether he rage or laugh, there is no rest.   _Proverbs 29:9_

Trouble

The righteous is delivered out of trouble, and the wicked cometh in his stead.   *Proverbs 11:8*

The merciful man doeth good to his own soul: but he that is cruel troubleth his own flesh.   *Proverbs 11:17*

He that troubleth his own house shall inherit the wind: and the fool shall be servant to the wise of heart.

Proverbs 11:29

The wicked is snared by the transgression of his lips: but the just shall come out of trouble.   *Proverbs 12:13*

In the house of the righteous is much treasure: but in the revenues of the wicked is trouble.   *Proverbs 15:6*

Better is little with the fear of the LORD than great treasure and trouble therewith.   *Proverbs 15:16*

He that is greedy of gain troubleth his own house; but he that hateth gifts shall live.   *Proverbs 15:27*

Whoso mocketh the poor reproacheth his Maker: and he that is glad at calamities shall not be unpunished.

Proverbs 17:5

A friend loveth at all times, and a brother is born for adversity. *Proverbs 17:17*

A foolish son is the calamity of his father: and the contentions of a wife are a continual dropping.

Proverbs 19:13

Whoso keepeth his mouth and his tongue keepeth his soul from troubles. *Proverbs 21:23*

If thou faint in the day of adversity, thy strength is small.

Proverbs 24:10

Confidence in an unfaithful man in time of trouble is like a broken tooth, and a foot out of joint. *Proverbs 25:19*

Trust

Trust in the LORD with all thine heart; and lean not unto thine own understanding. In all thy ways acknowledge him, and he shall direct thy paths. *Proverbs 3:5–6*

He that trusteth in his riches shall fall: but the righteous shall flourish as a branch. *Proverbs 11:28*

He that handleth a matter wisely shall find good: and whoso trusteth in the LORD, happy is he. *Proverbs 16:20*

Bow down thine ear, and hear the words of the wise, and apply thine heart unto my knowledge. For it is a pleasant thing if thou keep them within thee; they shall withal be fitted in thy lips. That thy trust may be in the LORD, I have made known to thee this day, even to thee. Have not I written to thee excellent things in counsels and knowledge, That I might make thee know the certainty of the words of truth; that thou mightest answer the words of truth to them that send unto thee? *Proverbs 22:17–21*

He that is of a proud heart stirreth up strife: but he that putteth his trust in the LORD shall be made fat.
Proverbs 28:25

Truth

Let not mercy and truth forsake thee: bind them about thy neck; write them upon the table of thine heart: So shalt thou find favour and good understanding in the sight of God and man.   *Proverbs 3:3–4*

Hear; for I will speak of excellent things; and the opening of my lips shall be right things. For my mouth shall speak truth; and wickedness is an abomination to my lips.

Proverbs 8:6–7

He that speaketh truth sheweth forth righteousness: but a false witness deceit.   *Proverbs 12:17*

The lip of truth shall be established for ever: but a lying tongue is but for a moment.   *Proverbs 12:19*

Lying lips are abomination to the Lord: but they that deal truly are his delight.   *Proverbs 12:22*

Do they not err that devise evil? but mercy and truth shall be to them that devise good.   *Proverbs 14:22*

A true witness delivereth souls: but a deceitful witness speaketh lies.   *Proverbs 14:25*

By mercy and truth iniquity is purged: and by the fear of the LORD men depart from evil.   *Proverbs 16:6*

Mercy and truth preserve the king: and his throne is upholden by mercy.   *Proverbs 20:28*

Have not I written to thee excellent things in counsels and knowledge, That I might make thee know the certainty of the words of truth; that thou mightest answer the words of truth to them that send unto thee?   *Proverbs 22:20–21*

Buy the truth, and sell it not; also wisdom, and instruction, and understanding.   *Proverbs 23:23*

Understanding

A wise man will hear, and will increase learning; and a man of understanding shall attain unto wise counsels

Proverbs 1:5

My son, if thou wilt receive my words, and hide my commandments with thee; So that thou incline thine ear unto wisdom, and apply thine heart to understanding; Yea, if thou criest after knowledge, and liftest up thy voice for understanding; If thou seekest her as silver, and searchest for her as for hid treasures; Then shalt thou understand the fear of the LORD, and find the knowledge of God.

Proverbs 2:1–5

For the LORD giveth wisdom: out of his mouth cometh knowledge and understanding. He layeth up sound wisdom for the righteous: he is a buckler to them that walk uprightly. He keepeth the paths of judgment, and preserveth the way of his saints. Then shalt thou understand righteousness, and judgment, and equity; yea, every good path. When wisdom entereth into thine heart, and knowledge is pleasant unto thy soul; Discretion shall preserve thee, understanding shall keep thee. *Proverbs 2:6–11*

Let not mercy and truth forsake thee: bind them about thy neck; write them upon the table of thine heart: So shalt thou find favour and good understanding in the sight of God and man. *Proverbs 3:3–4*

Trust in the LORD with all thine heart; and lean not unto thine own understanding. In all thy ways acknowledge him, and he shall direct thy paths.   *Proverbs 3:5–6*

Happy is the man that findeth wisdom, and the man that getteth understanding.   *Proverbs 3:13*

Hear, ye children, the instruction of a father, and attend to know understanding.   *Proverbs 4:1*

Get wisdom, get understanding: forget it not; neither decline from the words of my mouth. Forsake her not, and she shall preserve thee: love her, and she shall keep thee.
                    Proverbs 4:5–6

Wisdom is the principal thing; therefore get wisdom: and with all thy getting get understanding.   *Proverbs 4:7*

My son, attend unto my wisdom, and bow thine ear to my understanding: That thou mayest regard discretion, and that thy lips may keep knowledge.   *Proverbs 5:1–2*

But whoso committeth adultery with a woman lacketh understanding: he that doeth it destroyeth his own soul.
                    Proverbs 6:32

My son, keep my words, and lay up my commandments with thee. Keep my commandments, and live; and my law as the apple of thine eye. Bind them upon thy fingers, write them upon the table of thine heart. Say unto wisdom, Thou art my sister; and call understanding thy kinswoman: That they may keep thee from the strange woman, from the stranger which flattereth with her words.   *Proverbs 7:1–5*

Doth not wisdom cry? and understanding put forth her voice? She standeth in the top of high places, by the way in the places of the paths. She crieth at the gates, at the entry of the city, at the coming in at the doors. Unto you, O men, I call; and my voice is to the sons of man. O ye simple, understand wisdom: and, ye fools, be ye of an understanding heart.

Proverbs 8:1–5

All the words of my mouth are in righteousness; there is nothing froward or perverse in them. They are all plain to him that understandeth, and right to them that find knowledge. Receive my instruction, and not silver; and knowledge rather than choice gold.   Proverbs 8:8–10

Counsel is mine, and sound wisdom: I am understanding; I have strength. By me kings reign, and princes decree justice. By me princes rule, and nobles, even all the judges of the earth.   *Proverbs 8:15–16*

Wisdom hath builded her house, she hath hewn out her seven pillars: She hath killed her beasts; she hath mingled her wine; she hath also furnished her table. She hath sent forth her maidens: she crieth upon the highest places of the city, Whoso is simple, let him turn in hither: as for him that wanteth understanding, she saith to him, Come, eat of my bread, and drink of the wine which I have mingled. Forsake the foolish, and live; and go in the way of understanding.

Proverbs 9:1–6

In the lips of him that hath understanding wisdom is found: but a rod is for the back of him that is void of understanding. *Proverbs 10:13*

It is as sport to a fool to do mischief: but a man of understanding hath wisdom. *Proverbs 10:23*

He that is void of wisdom despiseth his neighbour: but a man of understanding holdeth his peace. *Proverbs 11:12*

He that tilleth his land shall be satisfied with bread: but he that followeth vain persons is void of understanding.

Proverbs 12:11

Good understanding giveth favour: but the way of transgressors is hard. *Proverbs 13:15*

A scorner seeketh wisdom, and findeth it not: but knowledge is easy unto him that understandeth.   *Proverbs 14:6*

The wisdom of the prudent is to understand his way: but the folly of fools is deceit.   *Proverbs 14:8*

He that is slow to wrath is of great understanding: but he that is hasty of spirit exalteth folly.   *Proverbs 14:29*

Wisdom resteth in the heart of him that hath understanding: but that which is in the midst of fools is made known.
     Proverbs 14:33

The heart of him that hath understanding seeketh knowledge: but the mouth of fools feedeth on foolishness.
     Proverbs 15:14

Folly is joy to him that is destitute of wisdom: but a man of understanding walketh uprightly.   *Proverbs 15:21*

He that refuseth instruction despiseth his own soul: but he that heareth reproof getteth understanding.
     Proverbs 15:32

How much better is it to get wisdom than gold! and to get understanding rather to be chosen than silver!
     Proverbs 16:16

Understanding is a wellspring of life unto him that hath it: but the instruction of fools is folly. *Proverbs 16:22*

A man void of understanding striketh hands, and becometh surety in the presence of his friend. *Proverbs 17:18*

Wisdom is before him that hath understanding; but the eyes of a fool are in the ends of the earth. *Proverbs 17:24*

He that hath knowledge spareth his words: and a man of understanding is of an excellent spirit. *Proverbs 17:27*

Even a fool, when he holdeth his peace, is counted wise: and he that shutteth his lips is esteemed a man of understanding. *Proverbs 17:28*

A fool hath no delight in understanding, but that his heart may discover itself. *Proverbs 18:2*

He that getteth wisdom loveth his own soul: he that keepeth understanding shall find good. *Proverbs 19:8*

Smite a scorner, and the simple will beware: and reprove one that hath understanding, and he will understand knowledge. *Proverbs 19:25*

Counsel in the heart of man is like deep water; but a man of understanding will draw it out.   *Proverbs 20:5*

Man's goings are of the LORD; how can a man then understand his own way?   *Proverbs 20:24*

The man that wandereth out of the way of understanding shall remain in the congregation of the dead.
            Proverbs 21:16

There is no wisdom nor understanding nor counsel against the LORD.   *Proverbs 21:30*

Buy the truth, and sell it not; also wisdom, and instruction, and understanding.   *Proverbs 23:23*

Through wisdom is an house builded; and by understanding it is established: And by knowledge shall the chambers be filled with all precious and pleasant riches.
            Proverbs 24:3–4

I went by the field of the slothful, and by the vineyard of the man void of understanding; And, lo, it was all grown over with thorns, and nettles had covered the face thereof, and the stone wall thereof was broken down.
            Proverbs 24:30–31

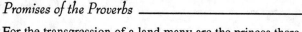

For the transgression of a land many are the princes thereof: but by a man of understanding and knowledge the state thereof shall be prolonged. *Proverbs 28:2*

Evil men understand not judgment: but they that seek the LORD understand all things. *Proverbs 28:5*

The rich man is wise in his own conceit; but the poor that hath understanding searcheth him out. *Proverbs 28:11*

The prince that wanteth understanding is also a great oppressor: but he that hateth covetousness shall prolong his days. *Proverbs 28:16*

The righteous considereth the cause of the poor: but the wicked regardeth not to know it. *Proverbs 29:7*

A servant will not be corrected by words: for though he understand he will not answer. *Proverbs 29:19*

The Wicked

For the upright shall dwell in the land, and the perfect shall remain in it. But the wicked shall be cut off from the earth, and the transgressors shall be rooted out of it.

Proverbs 2:21–22

The curse of the LORD is in the house of the wicked: but he blesseth the habitation of the just.　　　*Proverbs 3:33*

Enter not into the path of the wicked, and go not in the way of evil men. Avoid it, pass not by it, turn from it, and pass away.　　　*Proverbs 4:14–15*

The way of the wicked is as darkness: they know not at what they stumble.　　　*Proverbs 4:19*

His own iniquities shall take the wicked himself, and he shall be holden with the cords of his sins. He shall die without instruction; and in the greatness of his folly he shall go astray.　　　*Proverbs 5:22–23*

A naughty person, a wicked man, walketh with a froward mouth. He winketh with his eyes, he speaketh with his feet, he teacheth with his fingers; Frowardness is in his heart, he deviseth mischief continually; he soweth discord. Therefore shall his calamity come suddenly; suddenly shall he be broken without remedy.　　　*Proverbs 6:12–15*

He that reproveth a scorner getteth to himself shame: and he that rebuketh a wicked man getteth himself a blot. Reprove not a scorner, lest he hate thee: rebuke a wise man, and he will love thee. *Proverbs 9:7–8*

The LORD will not suffer the soul of the righteous to famish: but he casteth away the substance of the wicked.
Proverbs 10:3

Blessings are upon the head of the just: but violence covereth the mouth of the wicked. *Proverbs 10:6*

The memory of the just is blessed: but the name of the wicked shall rot. *Proverbs 10:7*

The mouth of a righteous man is a well of life: but violence covereth the mouth of the wicked. *Proverbs 10:11*

The labour of the righteous tendeth to life: the fruit of the wicked to sin. *Proverbs 10:16*

The tongue of the just is as choice silver: the heart of the wicked is little worth. *Proverbs 10:20*

The fear of the wicked, it shall come upon him: but the desire of the righteous shall be granted. *Proverbs 10:24*

As the whirlwind passeth, so is the wicked no more: but the righteous is an everlasting foundation.   *Proverbs 10:25*

The fear of the LORD prolongeth days: but the years of the wicked shall be shortened.   *Proverbs 10:27*

The hope of the righteous shall be gladness: but the expectation of the wicked shall perish.   *Proverbs 10:28*

The righteous shall never be removed: but the wicked shall not inhabit the earth.   *Proverbs 10:30*

The lips of the righteous know what is acceptable: but the mouth of the wicked speaketh frowardness.

Proverbs 10:32

The righteousness of the perfect shall direct his way: but the wicked shall fall by his own wickedness.

Proverbs 11:5

When a wicked man dieth, his expectation shall perish: and the hope of unjust men perisheth.   *Proverbs 11:7*

The righteous is delivered out of trouble, and the wicked cometh in his stead.   *Proverbs 11:8*

When it goeth well with the righteous, the city rejoiceth: and when the wicked perish, there is shouting.

Proverbs 11:10

By the blessing of the upright the city is exalted: but it is overthrown by the mouth of the wicked.   *Proverbs 11:11*

The wicked worketh a deceitful work: but to him that soweth righteousness shall be a sure reward.

Proverbs 11:18

Though hand join in hand, the wicked shall not be unpunished: but the seed of the righteous shall be delivered.

Proverbs 11:21

The desire of the righteous is only good: but the expectation of the wicked is wrath.   *Proverbs 11:23*

Behold, the righteous shall be recompensed in the earth: much more the wicked and the sinner.   *Proverbs 11:31*

The thoughts of the righteous are right: but the counsels of the wicked are deceit.   *Proverbs 12:5*

The words of the wicked are to lie in wait for blood: but the mouth of the upright shall deliver them.   *Proverbs 12:6*

The wicked are overthrown, and are not: but the house of the righteous shall stand. *Proverbs 12:7*

A righteous man regardeth the life of his beast: but the tender mercies of the wicked are cruel. *Proverbs 12:10*

The wicked desireth the net of evil men: but the root of the righteous yieldeth fruit. *Proverbs 12:12*

The wicked is snared by the transgression of his lips: but the just shall come out of trouble. *Proverbs 12:13*

There shall no evil happen to the just: but the wicked shall be filled with mischief. *Proverbs 12:21*

The righteous is more excellent than his neighbour: but the way of the wicked seduceth them. *Proverbs 12:26*

The light of the righteous rejoiceth: but the lamp of the wicked shall be put out. *Proverbs 13:9*

A wicked messenger falleth into mischief: but a faithful ambassador is health. *Proverbs 13:17*

The righteous eateth to the satisfying of his soul: but the belly of the wicked shall want. *Proverbs 13:25*

The house of the wicked shall be overthrown: but the tabernacle of the upright shall flourish.   *Proverbs 14:11*

The evil bow before the good; and the wicked at the gates of the righteous.   *Proverbs 14:19*

The wicked is driven away in his wickedness: but the righteous hath hope in his death.   *Proverbs 14:32*

In the house of the righteous is much treasure: but in the revenues of the wicked is trouble.   *Proverbs 15:6*

The sacrifice of the wicked is an abomination to the LORD: but the prayer of the upright is his delight.

Proverbs 15:8

The way of the wicked is an abomination unto the LORD: but he loveth him that followeth after righteousness.

Proverbs 15:9

The thoughts of the wicked are an abomination to the LORD: but the words of the pure are pleasant words.

Proverbs 15:26

The heart of the righteous studieth to answer: but the mouth of the wicked poureth out evil things.   *Proverbs 15:28*

The LORD is far from the wicked: but he heareth the prayer of the righteous. *Proverbs 15:29*

The LORD hath made all things for himself: yea, even the wicked for the day of evil. *Proverbs 16:4*

An ungodly man diggeth up evil: and in his lips there is as a burning fire. *Proverbs 16:27*

A wicked doer giveth heed to false lips; and a liar giveth ear to a naughty tongue. *Proverbs 17:4*

He that justifieth the wicked, and he that condemneth the just, even they both are abomination to the LORD. *Proverbs 17:15*

A wicked man taketh a gift out of the bosom to pervert the ways of judgment. *Proverbs 17:23*

When the wicked cometh, then cometh also contempt, and with ignominy reproach. *Proverbs 18:3*

It is not good to accept the person of the wicked, to overthrow the righteous in judgment. *Proverbs 18:5*

An ungodly witness scorneth judgment: and the mouth of the wicked devoureth iniquity. *Proverbs 19:28*

A wise king scattereth the wicked, and bringeth the wheel over them. *Proverbs 20:26*

An high look, and a proud heart, and the plowing of the wicked, is sin. *Proverbs 21:4*

The robbery of the wicked shall destroy them; because they refuse to do judgment. *Proverbs 21:7*

The soul of the wicked desireth evil: his neighbour findeth no favour in his eyes. *Proverbs 21:10*

The righteous man wisely considereth the house of the wicked: but God overthroweth the wicked for their wickedness. *Proverbs 21:12*

The wicked shall be a ransom for the righteous, and the transgressor for the upright. *Proverbs 21:18*

The sacrifice of the wicked is abomination: how much more, when he bringeth it with a wicked mind?

Proverbs 21:27

A wicked man hardeneth his face: but as for the upright, he directeth his way. *Proverbs 21:29*

Lay not wait, O wicked man, against the dwelling of the righteous; spoil not his resting place: For a just man falleth seven times, and riseth up again: but the wicked shall fall into mischief. *Proverbs 24:15–16*

Fret not thyself because of evil men, neither be thou envious at the wicked; For there shall be no reward to the evil man; the candle of the wicked shall be put out.
Proverbs 24:19–20

He that saith unto the wicked, Thou art righteous; him shall the people curse, nations shall abhor him
Proverbs 24:24

Take away the wicked from before the king, and his throne shall be established in righteousness. *Proverbs 25:5*

A righteous man falling down before the wicked is as a troubled fountain, and a corrupt spring. *Proverbs 25:26*

Whoso diggeth a pit shall fall therein: and he that rolleth a stone, it will return upon him. *Proverbs 26:27*

The wicked flee when no man pursueth: but the righteous are bold as a lion. *Proverbs 28:1*

They that forsake the law praise the wicked: but such as keep the law contend with them. *Proverbs 28:4*

When righteous men do rejoice, there is great glory: but when the wicked rise, a man is hidden. *Proverbs 28:12*

As a roaring lion, and a ranging bear; so is a wicked ruler over the poor people. *Proverbs 28:15*

When the wicked rise, men hide themselves: but when they perish, the righteous increase. *Proverbs 28:28*

When the righteous are in authority, the people rejoice: but when the wicked beareth rule, the people mourn. *Proverbs 29:2*

The righteous considereth the cause of the poor: but the wicked regardeth not to know it. *Proverbs 29:7*

Whoso is partner with a thief hateth his own soul: he heareth cursing, and bewrayeth it not. *Proverbs 29:24*

Wickedness

Enter not into the path of the wicked, and go not in the way of evil men. Avoid it, pass not by it, turn from it, and pass away. For they sleep not, except they have done mischief; and their sleep is taken away, unless they cause some to fall. For they eat the bread of wickedness, and drink the wine of violence. *Proverbs 4:14–17*

The righteousness of the perfect shall direct his way: but the wicked shall fall by his own wickedness.

Proverbs 11:5

A good man obtaineth favour of the LORD: but a man of wicked devices will he condemn. *Proverbs 12:2*

A man shall not be established by wickedness: but the root of the righteous shall not be moved. *Proverbs 12:3*

Righteousness keepeth him that is upright in the way: but wickedness overthroweth the sinner. *Proverbs 13:6*

He that is soon angry dealeth foolishly: and a man of wicked devices is hated. *Proverbs 14:17*

The wicked is driven away in his wickedness: but the righteous hath hope in his death.   *Proverbs 14:32*

It is an abomination to kings to commit wickedness: for the throne is established by righteousness.   *Proverbs 16:12*

The righteous man wisely considereth the house of the wicked: but God overthroweth the wicked for their wickedness.   *Proverbs 21:12*

Burning lips and a wicked heart are like a potsherd covered with silver dross.   *Proverbs 26:23*

Whose hatred is covered by deceit, his wickedness shall be shewed before the whole congregation.   *Proverbs 26:26*

Such is the way of an adulterous woman; she eateth, and wipeth her mouth, and saith, I have done no wickedness.   *Proverbs 30:20*

Wisdom

The fear of the LORD is the beginning of knowledge: but fools despise wisdom and instruction.   *Proverbs 1:7*

Wisdom crieth without; she uttereth her voice in the streets: She crieth in the chief place of concourse, in the openings of the gates: in the city she uttereth her words, saying, How long, ye simple ones, will ye love simplicity? and the scorners delight in their scorning, and fools hate knowledge? Turn you at my reproof: behold, I will pour out my spirit unto you, I will make known my words unto you. . .But ye have set at nought all my counsel, and would none of my reproof: I also will laugh at your calamity; I will mock when your fear cometh; When your fear cometh as desolation, and your destruction cometh as a whirlwind; when distress and anguish cometh upon you. Then shall they call upon me, but I will not answer; they shall seek me early, but they shall not find me: For that they hated knowledge, and did not choose the fear of the LORD: They would none of my counsel: they despised all my reproof. Therefore shall they eat of the fruit of their own way, and be filled with their own devices. For the turning away of the simple shall slay them, and the prosperity of fools shall destroy them. But whoso hearkeneth unto me shall dwell safely, and shall be quiet from fear of evil.   *Proverbs 1:20–23, 25, 33*

My son, if thou wilt receive my words, and hide my commandments with thee; So that thou incline thine ear unto wisdom, and apply thine heart to understanding; Yea, if thou criest after knowledge, and liftest up thy voice for understanding; If thou seekest her as silver, and searchest for her as for hid treasures; Then shalt thou understand the fear of the LORD, and find the knowledge of God. For the LORD giveth wisdom: out of his mouth cometh knowledge and understanding. He layeth up sound wisdom for the righteous: he is a buckler to them that walk uprightly. He keepeth the paths of judgment, and preserveth the way of his saints. Then shalt thou understand righteousness, and judgment, and equity; yea, every good path. When wisdom entereth into thine heart, and knowledge is pleasant unto thy soul; Discretion shall preserve thee, understanding shall keep thee: To deliver thee from the way of the evil man, from the man that speaketh froward things; Who leave the paths of uprightness, to walk in the ways of darkness; Who rejoice to do evil, and delight in the frowardness of the wicked; Whose ways are crooked, and they froward in their paths: To deliver thee from the strange woman, even from the stranger which flattereth with her words; Which forsaketh the guide of her youth, and forgetteth the covenant of her God. For her house inclineth unto death, and her paths unto the dead. None that go unto her return again, neither take they hold of the paths of life. That thou mayest walk in the way of good men, and keep the paths of the righteous. For the upright shall dwell in the land, and the perfect shall remain in it. But the wicked shall be cut off from the earth, and the transgressors shall be rooted out of it.

Proverbs 2:1–22

Be not wise in thine own eyes: fear the LORD, and depart from evil. It shall be health to thy navel, and marrow to thy bones.

Proverbs 3:7–8

Happy is the man that findeth wisdom, and the man that getteth understanding.   Proverbs 3:13

The LORD by wisdom hath founded the earth; by understanding hath he established the heavens.   *Proverbs 3:19*

My son, attend unto my wisdom, and bow thine ear to my understanding: That thou mayest regard discretion, and that thy lips may keep knowledge.   *Proverbs 5:1–2*

Say unto wisdom, Thou art my sister; and call understanding thy kinswoman: That they may keep thee from the strange woman, from the stranger which flattereth with her words.
                                        Proverbs 7:4–5

Doth not wisdom cry? and understanding put forth her voice? She standeth in the top of high places, by the way in the places of the paths. She crieth at the gates, at the entry of the city, at the coming in at the doors. Unto you, O men, I call; and my voice is to the sons of man. O ye simple, understand wisdom: and, ye fools, be ye of an understanding heart.
                                        Proverbs 8:1–5

For wisdom is better than rubies; and all the things that may be desired are not to be compared to it. I wisdom dwell with prudence, and find out knowledge of witty inventions.
                                        Proverbs 8:11–12

The fear of the LORD is the beginning of wisdom: and the knowledge of the holy is understanding. *Proverbs 9:1*

In the lips of him that hath understanding wisdom is found: but a rod is for the back of him that is void of understanding. *Proverbs 10:13*

The lips of the righteous feed many: but fools die for want of wisdom. *Proverbs 10:21*

It is as sport to a fool to do mischief: but a man of understanding hath wisdom. *Proverbs 10:23*

The mouth of the just bringeth forth wisdom: but the froward tongue shall be cut out. *Proverbs 10:31*

When pride cometh, then cometh shame: but with the lowly is wisdom. *Proverbs 11:2*

He that is void of wisdom despiseth his neighbour: but a man of understanding holdeth his peace. *Proverbs 11:12*

A man shall be commended according to his wisdom: but he that is of a perverse heart shall be despised.

Proverbs 12:8

Only by pride cometh contention: but with the well advised is wisdom. *Proverbs 13:10*

A scorner seeketh wisdom, and findeth it not: but knowledge is easy unto him that understandeth. *Proverbs 14:6*

The wisdom of the prudent is to understand his way: but the folly of fools is deceit. *Proverbs 14:8*

Wisdom resteth in the heart of him that hath understanding: but that which is in the midst of fools is made known. *Proverbs 14:33*

Folly is joy to him that is destitute of wisdom: but a man of understanding walketh uprightly. *Proverbs 15:21*

The fear of the LORD is the instruction of wisdom; and before honour is humility. *Proverbs 15:33*

How much better is it to get wisdom than gold! and to get understanding rather to be chosen than silver! *Proverbs 16:16*

Wherefore is there a price in the hand of a fool to get wisdom, seeing he hath no heart to it? *Proverbs 17:16*

Wisdom is before him that hath understanding; but the eyes of a fool are in the ends of the earth.   *Proverbs 17:24*

Through desire a man, having separated himself, seeketh and intermeddleth with all wisdom.   *Proverbs 18:1*

The words of a man's mouth are as deep waters, and the wellspring of wisdom as a flowing brook.   *Proverbs 18:4*

He that getteth wisdom loveth his own soul: he that keepeth understanding shall find good.   *Proverbs 19:8*

There is no wisdom nor understanding nor counsel against the LORD.   *Proverbs 21:30*

Labour not to be rich: cease from thine own wisdom.
     Proverbs 23:4

Speak not in the ears of a fool: for he will despise the wisdom of thy words.   *Proverbs 23:9*

Buy the truth, and sell it not; also wisdom, and instruction, and understanding.   *Proverbs 23:23*

Through wisdom is an house builded; and by understanding it is established. *Proverbs 24:3*

Wisdom is too high for a fool: he openeth not his mouth in the gate. *Proverbs 24:7*

My son, eat thou honey, because it is good; and the honeycomb, which is sweet to thy taste: So shall the knowledge of wisdom be unto thy soul: when thou hast found it, then there shall be a reward, and thy expectation shall not be cut off. *Proverbs 24:13–14*

Whoso loveth wisdom rejoiceth his father: but he that keepeth company with harlots spendeth his substance. *Proverbs 29:3*

The Wise

A wise man will hear, and will increase learning; and a man of understanding shall attain unto wise counsels

Proverbs 1:5

The wise shall inherit glory: but shame shall be the promotion of fools.

Proverbs 3:35

Reprove not a scorner, lest he hate thee: rebuke a wise man, and he will love thee.

Proverbs 9:8

Give instruction to a wise man, and he will be yet wiser: teach a just man, and he will increase in learning.

Proverbs 9:9

If thou be wise, thou shalt be wise for thyself: but if thou scornest, thou alone shalt bear it.

Proverbs 9:12

The wise in heart will receive commandments: but a prating fool shall fall.

Proverbs 10:8

Wise men lay up knowledge: but the mouth of the foolish is near destruction.

Proverbs 10:14

In the multitude of words there wanteth not sin: but he that refraineth his lips is wise. *Proverbs 10:19*

He that troubleth his own house shall inherit the wind: and the fool shall be servant to the wise of heart.
Proverbs 11:29

The fruit of the righteous is a tree of life; and he that winneth souls is wise. *Proverbs 11:30*

The way of a fool is right in his own eyes: but he that hearkeneth unto counsel is wise. *Proverbs 12:15*

There is that speaketh like the piercings of a sword: but the tongue of the wise is health. *Proverbs 12:18*

A wise son heareth his father's instruction: but a scorner heareth not rebuke. *Proverbs 13:1*

The law of the wise is a fountain of life, to depart from the snares of death. *Proverbs 13:14*

He that walketh with wise men shall be wise: but a companion of fools shall be destroyed. *Proverbs 13:20*

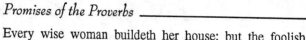

Every wise woman buildeth her house: but the foolish plucketh it down with her hands.   *Proverbs 14:1*

In the mouth of the foolish is a rod of pride: but the lips of the wise shall preserve them.   *Proverbs 14:3*

A wise man feareth, and departeth from evil: but the fool rageth, and is confident.   *Proverbs 14:16*

The crown of the wise is their riches: but the foolishness of fools is folly.   *Proverbs 14:24*

The king's favour is toward a wise servant: but his wrath is against him that causeth shame.   *Proverbs 14:35*

The tongue of the wise useth knowledge aright: but the mouth of fools poureth out foolishness.   *Proverbs 15:2*

The lips of the wise disperse knowledge: but the heart of the foolish doeth not so.   *Proverbs 15:7*

A scorner loveth not one that reproveth him: neither will he go unto the wise.   *Proverbs 15:12*

A wise son maketh a glad father: but a foolish man despiseth his mother.   *Proverbs 15:20*

The way of life is above to the wise, that he may depart from hell beneath. *Proverbs 15:24*

The ear that heareth the reproof of life abideth among the wise. *Proverbs 15:31*

The wrath of a king is as messengers of death: but a wise man will pacify it. *Proverbs 16:14*

He that handleth a matter wisely shall find good: and whoso trusteth in the LORD, happy is he. *Proverbs 16:20*

The wise in heart shall be called prudent: and the sweetness of the lips increaseth learning. *Proverbs 16:21*

The heart of the wise teacheth his mouth, and addeth learning to his lips. *Proverbs 16:23*

A wise servant shall have rule over a son that causeth shame, and shall have part of the inheritance among the brethren. *Proverbs 17:2*

A reproof entereth more into a wise man than an hundred stripes into a fool. *Proverbs 17:10*

The heart of the prudent getteth knowledge; and the ear of the wise seeketh knowledge. *Proverbs 18:15*

Hear counsel, and receive instruction, that thou mayest be wise in thy latter end. *Proverbs 19:20*

Wine is a mocker, strong drink is raging: and whosoever is deceived thereby is not wise. *Proverbs 20:1*

A wise king scattereth the wicked, and bringeth the wheel over them. *Proverbs 20:26*

When the scorner is punished, the simple is made wise: and when the wise is instructed, he receiveth knowledge.
Proverbs 21:11

There is treasure to be desired and oil in the dwelling of the wise; but a foolish man spendeth it up. *Proverbs 21:20*

A wise man scaleth the city of the mighty, and casteth down the strength of the confidence thereof. *Proverbs 21:22*

Bow down thine ear, and hear the words of the wise, and apply thine heart unto my knowledge. For it is a pleasant thing if thou keep them within thee; they shall withal be fitted in thy lips. *Proverbs 22:17–18*

My son, if thine heart be wise, my heart shall rejoice, even mine. Yea, my reins shall rejoice, when thy lips speak right things.   *Proverbs 23:15–16*

Hear thou, my son, and be wise, and guide thine heart in the way.   *Proverbs 23:19*

The father of the righteous shall greatly rejoice: and he that begetteth a wise child shall have joy of him. Thy father and thy mother shall be glad, and she that bare thee shall rejoice.   *Proverbs 23:24–25*

A wise man is strong; yea, a man of knowledge increaseth strength. For by wise counsel thou shalt make thy war: and in multitude of counsellors there is safety.
                                                    Proverbs 24:5–6

These things also belong to the wise. It is not good to have respect of persons in judgment.   *Proverbs 24:23*

As an earring of gold, and an ornament of fine gold, so is a wise reprover upon an obedient ear.   *Proverbs 25:12*

Answer a fool according to his folly, lest he be wise in his own conceit.   *Proverbs 26:5*

Seest thou a man wise in his own conceit? there is more hope of a fool than of him. *Proverbs 26:12*

My son, be wise, and make my heart glad, that I may answer him that reproacheth me. *Proverbs 27:11*

Whoso keepeth the law is a wise son: but he that is a companion of riotous men shameth his father. *Proverbs 28:7*

The rich man is wise in his own conceit; but the poor that hath understanding searcheth him out. *Proverbs 28:11*

Scornful men bring a city into a snare: but wise men turn away wrath. *Proverbs 29:8*

Woman

Drink waters out of thine own cistern, and running waters out of thine own well. Let thy fountains be dispersed abroad, and rivers of waters in the streets. Let them be only thine own, and not strangers' with thee. Let thy fountain be blessed: and rejoice with the wife of thy youth. Let her be as the loving hind and pleasant roe; let her breasts satisfy thee at all times; and be thou ravished always with her love. And why wilt thou, my son, be ravished with a strange woman, and embrace the bosom of a stranger?   *Proverbs 5:15–20*

But whoso committeth adultery with a woman lacketh understanding: he that doeth it destroyeth his own soul.
Proverbs 6:32

A foolish woman is clamorous: she is simple, and knoweth nothing.   *Proverbs 9:13*

A gracious woman retaineth honour: and strong men retain riches.   *Proverbs 11:16*

As a jewel of gold in a swine's snout, so is a fair woman which is without discretion.   *Proverbs 11:22*

A virtuous woman is a crown to her husband: but she that maketh ashamed is as rottenness in his bones.

Proverbs 12:4

Every wise woman buildeth her house: but the foolish plucketh it down with her hands.   *Proverbs 14:1*

Whoso findeth a wife findeth a good thing, and obtaineth favour of the LORD.   *Proverbs 18:22*

A foolish son is the calamity of his father: and the contentions of a wife are a continual dropping.

Proverbs 19:13

It is better to dwell in a corner of the housetop, than with a brawling woman in a wide house.   *Proverbs 21:9*

It is better to dwell in the wilderness, than with a contentious and an angry woman.   *Proverbs 21:19*

It is better to dwell in the corner of the housetop, than with a brawling woman and in a wide house.   *Proverbs 25:24*

A continual dropping in a very rainy day and a contentious woman are alike. Whosoever hideth her hideth the wind, and the ointment of his right hand, which bewrayeth itself.

Proverbs 27:15–16

Give not thy strength unto women, nor thy ways to that which destroyeth kings.   *Proverbs 31: 3*

Who can find a virtuous woman? for her price is far above rubies.   *Proverbs 31:10*

The heart of her husband doth safely trust in her, so that he shall have no need of spoil.   *Proverbs 31:11*

She will do him good and not evil all the days of her life.   *Proverbs 31:12*

She seeketh wool, and flax, and worketh willingly with her hands.   *Proverbs 31:13*

She is like the merchants' ships; she bringeth her food from afar.   *Proverbs 31:14*

She riseth also while it is yet night, and giveth meat to her household, and a portion to her maidens.   *Proverbs 31:15*

She considereth a field, and buyeth it: with the fruit of her hands she planteth a vineyard.   *Proverbs 31:16*

She girdeth her loins with strength, and strengtheneth her arms.   *Proverbs 31:17*

She perceiveth that her merchandise is good: her candle goeth not out by night.   *Proverbs 31:18*

She layeth her hands to the spindle, and her hands hold the distaff.   *Proverbs 31:19*

She stretcheth out her hand to the poor; yea, she reacheth forth her hands to the needy.   *Proverbs 31:20*

She is not afraid of the snow for her household: for all her household are clothed with scarlet.   *Proverbs 31:21*

She maketh herself coverings of tapestry; her clothing is silk and purple.   *Proverbs 31:22*

Her husband is known in the gates, when he sitteth among the elders of the land.   *Proverbs 31:23*

She maketh fine linen, and selleth it; and delivereth girdles unto the merchant.   *Proverbs 31:24*

Strength and honour are her clothing; and she shall rejoice in time to come.   *Proverbs 31:25*

She openeth her mouth with wisdom; and in her tongue is the law of kindness.   *Proverbs 31:26*

She looketh well to the ways of her household, and eateth not the bread of idleness.   *Proverbs 31:27*

Her children arise up, and call her blessed; her husband also, and he praiseth her.   *Proverbs 31:28*

Many daughters have done virtuously, but thou excellest them all.   *Proverbs 31:29*

Favour is deceitful, and beauty is vain: but a woman that feareth the LORD, she shall be praised.   *Proverbs 31:30*

Give her of the fruit of her hands; and let her own works praise her in the gates.   *Proverbs 31:31*

Work

He becometh poor that dealeth with a slack hand: but the hand of the diligent maketh rich.   *Proverbs 10:4*

He that gathereth in summer is a wise son: but he that sleepeth in harvest is a son that causeth shame.

Proverbs 10:5

The labour of the righteous tendeth to life: the fruit of the wicked to sin.   *Proverbs 10:16*

The wicked worketh a deceitful work: but to him that soweth righteousness shall be a sure reward.

Proverbs 11:18

He that tilleth his land shall be satisfied with bread: but he that followeth vain persons is void of understanding.

Proverbs 12:11

A man shall be satisfied with good by the fruit of his mouth: and the recompence of a man's hands shall be rendered unto him.   *Proverbs 12:14*

The hand of the diligent shall bear rule: but the slothful shall be under tribute.   *Proverbs 12:24*

The slothful man roasteth not that which he took in hunting: but the substance of a diligent man is precious.
Proverbs 12:27

Wealth gotten by vanity shall be diminished: but he that gathereth by labour shall increase. *Proverbs 13:11*

Where no oxen are, the crib is clean: but much increase is by the strength of the ox. *Proverbs 14:4*

In all labour there is profit: but the talk of the lips tendeth only to penury. *Proverbs 14:23*

Commit thy works unto the LORD, and thy thoughts shall be established. *Proverbs 16:3*

He that laboureth laboureth for himself; for his mouth craveth it of him. *Proverbs 16:26*

He also that is slothful in his work is brother to him that is a great waster. *Proverbs 18:9*

Even a child is known by his doings, whether his work be pure, and whether it be right. *Proverbs 20:11*

The way of man is froward and strange: but as for the pure, his work is right.   *Proverbs 21:8*

It is joy to the just to do judgment: but destruction shall be to the workers of iniquity.   *Proverbs 21:15*

Seest thou a man diligent in his business? he shall stand before kings; he shall not stand before mean men.
                                        Proverbs 22:29

Labour not to be rich: cease from thine own wisdom.
                                        Proverbs 23:4

Prepare thy work without, and make it fit for thyself in the field; and afterwards build thine house.   *Proverbs 24:27*

Say not, I will do so to him as he hath done to me: I will render to the man according to his work.   *Proverbs 24:29*